Performance Management in Schools

2007

TES

Leadership skills in education management

Other titles in this series

The Head Teacher in the 21st Century
Being a successful school leader
by Frank Green

Mastering Deputy Headship
Acquiring the skills for future leadership
by Trevor Kerry

From Teacher to Middle Manager
Making the next step
by Susan Tranter

The Special Educational Needs Coordinator
Maximising your potential
by Vic Shuttleworth

Effective Classroom Teacher
Developing the skills you need in today's classroom
by Trevor Kerry and Mandy Wilding

Forthcoming

Middle Leadership in Schools
by Sonia Blandford

Performance Management in Schools

Unlocking your Team Potential

Susan Tranter and Adrian Percival

PEARSON
Longman

Harlow, England • London • New York • Boston • San Francisco • Toronto
Sydney • Tokyo • Singapore • Hong Kong • Seoul • Taipei • New Delhi
Cape Town • Madrid • Mexico City • Amsterdam • Munich • Paris • Milan

PEARSON EDUCATION LIMITED

Edinburgh Gate
Harlow CM20 2JE
Tel: +44 (0)1279 623623
Fax: +44 (0)1279 431059
Website: www.pearsoned.co.uk

First published in Great Britain 2006

ISBN-13: 978-1-4058-1237-5
ISBN-10: 1-4058-1237-0

British Library Cataloguing-in-Publication Data
A catalogue record for this book is available from the British Library

Library of Congress Cataloging-in-Publication Data
Tranter, Susan.
    Performance management in schools : unlocking your team potential / Susan Tranter and Adrian Percival.
        p. cm.
    Includes bibliograhical references and index.
    ISBN-13: 978–1–4058–1237–5 (pbk. : alk. paper)
    ISBN-10: 1–4058–1237–0 (pbk. : alk. paper)
    1. Teachers—Rating of—Great Britain.   2. Teacher effectiveness—Great Britain.   I. Percival, Adrian, MSc.   II. Title.

LB2838.T72 2006
371.14′40941—dc22

2005055295

10 9   8   7   6   5 4 3 2 1
10 09 08 07 06

Typeset in 10.5/14pt Latin 725BT by 35
Printed and bound in Great Britain by Henry Ling Ltd., at the Dorset Press, Dorchester, Dorset

The publisher's policy is to use paper manufactured from sustainable forests.

SUSAN TRANTER is Headteacher of Fitzharrys School in Abingdon, a specialist technology college. Previously Susan was associate Headteacher of Matthew Arnold School, where Adrian Percival was Executive Headteacher of the Federation. During their time working together Matthew Arnold became one of the most improved schools in the country. Susan worked as a consultant school leader in a school of concern, a secondment that helped to raise attainment, improved curriculum monitoring and provided leadership consultancy to members of the leadership team.

Susan has worked in a range of secondary schools including single sex, grammar, secondary modern and comprehensive. Her responsibilities have included head of sixth form, head of mathematics, primary liaison, teaching and learning; she has postgraduate degrees in Pure Mathematics and Management in Education. More recently she was one of the first to complete the NPQH. Susan is author of *From Teacher to Middle Manager* (Pearson (2000)) and *Diary of a Deputy* (Routledge (2002)). Susan is a research associate for the NCSL researching top talent programmes and performance management – her 'Hotseat' was one of the most popular to date with nearly 6000 'hits'. Susan was recently a guest speaker at the NCSL's Leading Edge conference on Growing Leadership Potential and at the SST/SHA conference on Personalised Learning. Susan wrote a paper for the iNET conference on the student voice in education.

ADRIAN PERCIVAL is the National School Improvement Partner Coordinator working as part of the National Strategies team. In this role he has responsibility for the leadership of the SIP programme and for ensuring that DfES policies are effectively put into practice across the country. Prior to this national role Adrian worked in schools for 18 years in a teaching career spanning Staffordshire, where he taught physics; Berkshire, where he worked in a variety of roles including GNVQ coordinator setting up the first GNVQ courses in the county; Surrey, where he was deputy head of France Hill School and Oxfordshire where he was head of Matthew Arnold School in Oxford.

Matthew Arnold was an underachieving school that was on the edge of an Ofsted category as a result of the inspection that took place in Adrian's second week there. In his six years at the school GCSE results rose consistently year-on-year from 43 percent 5+ A*–C in 1999 to 71 percent in 2005. The school achieved specialist status in science in the first round of this specialism and soon became a leading specialist school within the movement.

Outside his work with these schools, Adrian has published texts for physics up to GCSE and has published articles in *Managing Schools Today* and the SHA journal *Headlines*.

As a team

Having piloted a leadership development course for the Specialist Schools Trust (SST), Adrian and Susan were commissioned to produce a series of Teach and Learn Units in collaboration between the SST, BBC and Open University.

Susan Tranter and Adrian Percival co-wrote *How to Run a School Successfully* published by Continuum in 2004.

Contents

List of tables   x
List of figures   xi
Preface   xiii

1 The changing face of schools   1

   Why performance management for teachers?   2
   Performance management for support staff   8
   A new school culture   10
   Making it work   11
   Conclusion   14

2 Creating the policy   17

   Creating a policy   21
   Elements of the policy   23
   Lesson observation   34
   Other staff and workforce reform   35
   Conclusion   36

3 The coaching paradigm   39

   Meetings   40
   The coaching model in action   42
   The benefits of the coaching paradigm   54
   Conclusion   55

4 Creating job descriptions   57

   The legal position   58
   Creating an effective job description   61
   Title of the job   61

Grading and pay   67
Core purpose   68
From core purpose to specifics   70
Support staff   75
Conclusion   77

5 Headteacher performance management   81

Making headteacher performance management work   83
The school improvement partner   85
Objective setting   87
Monitoring the objectives   90
Conclusion   94

6 Looking after the support staff   97

What will the support staff do?   100
Where will the support staff work?   104
Managing performance   105
Setting and reviewing objectives   108
Conclusion   113

7 Assessing progress   115

How to get going   117
What to talk about   123
How to keep records   127
The formal annual review   128
360-degree feedback   136
Working with people   140
Conclusion   142

8 Linking staff development to performance
  management   145

Reflection and critical incidents   146
Feedback   151
Keeping a personal portfolio   152
Linking performance management to training
and development   152
Conclusion   157

9 The future of performance management 159

Leadership programmes 161
Competencies and behaviours 165
Teamwork 167
Conclusion 168

Appendix: Sample job descriptions 171

Director of staff development 172
Head of subject 177
Year leader 180
Classroom teacher 183
Curriculum administrator 188

Index 190

List of tables

1.1 Key steps in performance management 4

4.1 Setting the TLR tariff 73

6.1 Sample job description for assessment administrator 103

6.2 Annual review for administration personnel 110

7.1 Review and planning timetable 120

7.2 Summary notes 129

7.3 Feedback form 139

List of figures

1.1   Maslow's hierarchy of needs   12

3.1   Situational leadership   43

7.1   Performance management cycle   119

7.2   Residual analysis for English   131

7.3   Residual analysis by set and gender   131

Preface

In recent years the rate of change in schools has accelerated beyond what few could have imagined 15 years ago. The changes are both in the nature of the workplace and in the nature of accountability of those working in schools. The workforce in schools is increasingly diverse, with more and more support staff carrying out functions for which previously only teachers would have been used. For instance, in the early days of information technology (IT) in schools there would have been an enthusiastic teacher who would have developed the expertise to manage the network, without the help of any support staff. It was certainly expected that teachers would administer all exams, and many people still believe that only teachers should invigilate. The revolution is proceeding so fast that now those not trained as teachers are expected to supervise classes when the class teacher is absent, and even, in some cases, the pastoral management of pupils is delegated to those not trained as teachers. Who would have expected things to turn out this way even five years ago? As well as this radical shift in the workforce there is the ever increasing accountability that schools face. Thirty years ago, before the school effectiveness movement was launched by Rutter et al. (1979) in their seminal work *Fifteen Thousand Hours*, schools were largely regarded as irrelevant to the achievement of their pupils. Achievement was believed to be determined solely by external factors. Fortunately today (despite the urgings of some of the more extreme commentators on the right wing) we have not moved to the position where external factors are disregarded altogether, but we are securely in a place where schools are regarded as having a significant effect upon educational outcomes. With that realisation has come regular inspections of schools by the Office for Standards in Education (Ofsted), performance tables, the school Performance and Assessment Report (PANDA) and, most recently, the analysis of school performance provided by the Fischer Family Trust, which is based on factors such as prior attainment, special needs, ethnic group and so on.

There is no hiding place for schools in the increasingly accountable educational world in which we live.

For these reasons schools have been forced to develop their principles of leadership and management of the workforce to be at the cutting edge in these areas. Gone are the days when schools would go to the private sector in commerce and industry for advice about how they could improve their skills. Certainly there is still much to be learnt from these sectors, but no longer do we look to the private sector to teach us: we learn from each other. Leadership is the vogue in schools. It is recognised broadly as the key determinant of successful schools. The establishment of the National College for School Leadership in 2000 provided high-profile backing from government for the importance of school leadership, and more recently the introduction of the New Relationship with Schools in 2005, with the pivotal role played by school improvement partners in this relationship, showed the priority placed on investing in leadership in schools and on providing the correct level of challenge and support from those who are already successful school leaders.

Within this context we believe that performance management has a crucial role to play. In some schools performance management is just another centrally imposed burden; in these schools the prophecy is self-fulfilling – no one sees the benefit of performance management because it is not expected to have any benefit. In other schools performance management is the core of their approach to school improvement. We believe that the latter position is attainable by all who really want it. The purpose of this book is to show how to make performance management not an activity that must be completed (typically by allocating a bit of time on an in-service training – INSET – day), but rather a way of life in the workplace. Performance management is, at the risk of providing a tautology, all about managing performance, and this is something that must concern everyone who cares about the success of their school. In our view performance management rests upon two principles. The first is that managers can have a reasonable expectation that those they manage will do the best job they can and should welcome the opportunity for a dialogue aimed at helping them improve the standard of their work. The second is that all those who work in an organisation have the right to expect a process of management and development that will enable them to carry out their work to the best of their ability; in other words, if there is an aspect of their work that is lacking, they have the right to the support needed to improve.

At the beginning of this preface we indicated that the rate of change has gone beyond anything anyone could have expected 15 years ago. The reason for choosing this particular time span is that it includes the introduction of statutory appraisal for teachers. This was the first serious attempt to introduce, on a national level, the idea that teachers should expect to be managed by their managers. However, for whatever reason, the whole appraisal process was diverted off into something of a cul-de-sac, resulting in cosy chats every two years between teachers who did not necessarily have any line management relationship – if it happened at all. We believe the development of the appraisal system, and its subsequent replacement by the current performance management system, is instructive for the development of our processes and procedures for performance management in the future. An examination of this move from appraisal to performance management forms the substance of the first chapter of this book.

Having considered the broad aims of performance management, we need to move on to implementation. One of the difficulties with performance management is that it is a system that operates confidentially between the manager and the managed. Consequently it is difficult to monitor and evaluate the true impact of the process. The policy developed must be mindful of this difficulty and must provide a robust vehicle for ensuring that performance management takes place, and that it takes place effectively. Clearly part of this must be the extent to which those affected by the policy are engaged in drawing it up. The second chapter tackles the issues of engagement in the policy and some of the pitfalls to avoid in its creation.

At its heart, successful performance management is about the dialogue between two people – the manager and the managed. Chapter 3 provides a conceptual framework for conducting that dialogue. It is easy to come up with diagrams and theories for effective practice, but rather more difficult to imagine those models in practice. For this reason a substantial part of Chapter 3 focuses upon case studies of the framework in practice, with team members presenting very different challenges to their managers.

Any text on performance management will tell us that the process starts with a job description. Chapter 4 is therefore an in-depth consideration of how job descriptions may be framed to be most helpful both to the holder of the job description and to the person who manages the performance of that person. We are particularly keen to emphasise the extent to which jobs should not only be specified in terms of the tasks and activities expected of the person, but also the outcomes that are expected. Too often outcomes are ignored in favour of activity, but successful performance management considers the impact that the person makes above all else.

The headteacher in a school is in a curious position because there is no line manager for the head. There is no sense in which the head can be performance-managed in the same way as everyone else. Most people expect their performance management to be carried out by someone who knows their work and has expertise in that area of activity. Generally, and in very simple terms, the way people move up the ladder is by being good at the previous step, and so when it comes to performance management of their team they have a basis in expertise from having done that job or one similar to it. This is not the case for the head, whose performance management is carried out by a committee of the governors. These governors have no expertise in the work of the head and may or may not have a knowledge of the head's work. Governors are therefore provided with expert advice from an external adviser (until 2005–6, or a school improvement partner – SIP – thereafter). There are particular challenges here for the head and the governors. Chapter 5 provides some guidance through some of the issues they may face.

Since schools employ an increasingly diverse workforce, and the lines of responsibility are increasingly blurred, we believe it is essential that we always consider the staff as a whole. Although there are still teachers who refer to 'the staff' and mean only the teachers, we hope that these colleagues are becoming increasingly few and far between. We aim for a fully integrated workforce where all staff have the same entitlements. The performance management legislation only applies to teachers, but we believe that it is about good practice in employment and so *all* staff should benefit. However, we do need to consider how the performance management process needs to be tailored to the work of the employee: a straight transplant of the teacher's statutory process will not suffice. Chapter 6 explores the issues surrounding performance management of support staff.

Performance management is about setting objectives and then achieving those objectives. Unless the objectives are very simple (and therefore possibly unsuitable as objectives) then measuring progress towards them is going to be potentially problematic. Chapter 7 provides some tools for assessing progress.

Ultimately people only become more effective at work if they wish to. Personal reflection is critical to improved performance, and this is why so many performance management and appraisal policies place self-evaluation at the heart of the process. Learning to be self-critical and reflective is the most important part of improving our own performance. Chapter 8 therefore provides some concepts and tools that together create a framework for self-evaluation.

Finally, in Chapter 9 we consider the way forward. Is performance management slowly but surely evolving (or regressing) into the appraisal system that it has replaced? What do we need to do to ensure this does not happen? Ultimately our contention is that performance management works and brings about rapid improvement where managers are prepared to provide colleagues with frank and developmental feedback on their performance. Where managers avoid the issue – or worse, use the process to provide colleagues with an opportunity for a good old moan – then performance management provides no value whatsoever. This final chapter will provide some thoughts on warning signs to look out for in your own procedure.

Performance management is the answer to school improvement if its potential is fully realised. To achieve this means that we can never consider the job done, the policy in place – performance management requires continual monitoring and skill development for those engaged in the process. Performance management is not an easy prescription for improvement but we are convinced that it does work, and that we hope some of the thoughts presented in this book will help make your performance management system even more successful in producing the outcomes you desire.

Reference

Rutter, M., Maughan, B., Mortimore, P. and Ouston, J. (1979) *Fifteen Thousand Hours: Secondary Schools and their Effects on Children*, Open Books, London.

chapter one

The changing face of schools

Why performance management for teachers?

Performance management for support staff

A new school culture

Making it work

Conclusion

Schools are very different organisations compared to 30 years ago. Long gone are the days of the individual teacher determining the curriculum for their class and then how they should go about teaching it. Teachers now work as part of extended teams where each teacher must contribute to the performance of the team as a whole and where a high priority is placed upon consistent practice and shared planning. The individual interaction between teacher and pupil is increasingly regarded as a source of potential variability. Teams have team leaders accountable for the performance and results of their team. Heads of department are leaders of teaching and learning, not administrators of resources, and as team leaders they have responsibility for managing and leading their teams.

The typical school staff of the modern school will now include a whole range of para-professionals, including curriculum administration assistants, assessment administrators, reprographics technicians, whole teams of IT technicians, staff to deal with examination administration, teaching assistants (barely heard of 30 years ago), cover assistants, counsellors, pupil learning assistants and many more. All these people support the work of teachers in class, replacing what might just have been a school secretary and a science technician. These new work patterns and the new work-force require new ways of working in schools. And this is where performance management comes in. Of course, teachers in schools have to function within a statutory framework of performance management, as described in Chapter 2 of this book. Because of the statutory nature of performance management for teachers, it deserves separate treatment from the highly desirable, but non-statutory performance management that we will recommend for support staff in school.

Why performance management for teachers?

For many years teachers have overemphasised the idea of 'professionalism'. In this analysis the teacher is rather like a doctor, operating as an individual professional within the school (or 'practice'): as a 'professional' the teacher is an autonomous worker with an accountability to the client (pupil? parent?) and takes steps to ensure that the correct treatment is provided to address the diagnosis of what the pupil needs. The professional teacher can be relied upon to act at all times in the best interests of the pupil and, furthermore, is suitably trained, skilled and qualified to know exactly what is within the pupil's best interests. The professional teacher is able to apply their skills to help the pupil learn to best effect. Perhaps this description verges on caricature, but it is fair to say that the spirit of teacher professionalism does cast a long shadow over attempts to raise standards in schools.

The first attempt at introducing serious accountability for teachers was the appraisal regulations brought in by statutory instrument in 1991. Under these regulations each teacher had a two-year appraisal cycle, involving two observations (lasting around one hour in total) and a review meeting where the previously agreed focus for appraisal could be discussed. Perhaps because of the potentially cataclysmic effect the mention of appraisal had on some teachers and school leaders there was a considerable effort put into marketing the process. It was presented as being principally about professional development and not about making judgements about colleagues. As Bennett (1999) noted: 'In introducing appraisal, some schools have been appraisee-centred to the exclusion of a school dimension' (p. 413).

Perhaps as a consequence of this – and of the very rapid change in the culture of schools throughout the 1990s – it became clear that towards the latter half of that decade the existing appraisal regulations were out of step with the times. Bartlett (1998) captures the mood of the time well:

Many evaluations carried out since its introduction have sought to show how appraisal may be part of the process of increasing school effectiveness [. . .]. Whilst illustrating how appraisal can be beneficial in terms of whole-school outcomes, these studies have also pointed out the rather patchy nature of its introduction nationally. Others have been much stronger in criticising the lack of concrete outcomes from the early experiences of appraisal [. . .]. Woodhead (1996), the Chief Inspector of Education, called for a more rigorous process, less shrouded in confidentiality, with more focused target-setting. Shephard (1996), whilst Secretary of State for Education, would like to have seen an appraisal process with 'teeth'. (pp. 479–80)

In short, there was a view that the appraisal process that had been introduced as a form of sharpened accountability for teachers had been subverted into a series of cosy chats. As a deputy head quoted by Bartlett put it:

If the Government had had the power to set a much tougher system up, they would have done so, but they didn't have that power. So they had to put in a half-baked system which they could get away with . . . it's one of those things where you're forced to do it but nobody checks up to see if you have done it. (p. 481)

Performance management for teachers could be interpreted as a direct attack on the notion of the teacher as professional. The long shadow referred to above is most evident when teachers are asked to manage and in particular when they are asked to 'judge' other teachers. There are few tasks that make teachers recoil more quickly than having to judge their colleagues. This is odd, given that they are in the business of providing judgement on the work of others: they are generally more than happy to provide appropriate feedback to their pupils on where they have gone wrong and what they could do to improve (indeed some are all to happy to provide on occasion inappropriate feedback too!). But when it comes to their co-workers then this willingness departs very rapidly. Why do teachers find this such an irksome responsibility? One possibility is the view that there are no right or wrong ways to teach, there are just different ways, and that as a consequence no teacher is in a position to sit in judgement on another as they are all equally qualified and equally professional. This (admittedly polarised) analysis is what led to the original forms of teacher appraisal that were set up in the statutory framework described above. The framework was based clearly on the paradigm of teacher as professional with the emphasis placed entirely upon professional development in the cosiest sense of the phrase. Performance management requires an entirely new mindset. It sets out in a straightforward way that teachers have line managers and that these line managers should review the work of those they manage on a regular basis. The result of these reviews will be a celebration of strengths but should also provide a series of clearly defined areas for improvement.

In contrast to the previous appraisal framework the new performance management regulations had a much clearer set of expectations about how the whole process would work. Table 1.1 is reproduced from *Performance Management in Schools* (DfES, 2000).

TABLE 1.1 Key steps in performance management

Making a commitment	Committing the school to performance management. Research shows that the management team need to model the type of performance management behaviour they wish teachers to demonstrate.
Defining roles	Deciding who is responsible for the development and implementation of the policy, as well as responsibilities for individuals' performance.

TABLE 1.1   (cont'd)

Agreeing responsibilities and timetable	Setting out when and how all teachers are involved. Linking the timetable with the school's planning cycle and existing arrangements to monitor progress and improvement within the school.
Agreeing policy and standard documents	Agreeing what standard proformas should be used by all teachers for individual plans and for classroom observation.
Planning and setting objectives	This will include discussing: ■ other school planning processes that should be taken into account in formulating individual objectives; ■ what support is needed to meet objectives; ■ how professional development objectives will relate to the school's overall priorities for staff development.
Monitoring progress	This will include discussing: ■ informal arrangements for monitoring in-year, to ensure that progress and development needs are reviewed and team leaders and teachers gather enough information to discuss overall performance; ■ clear criteria for handling classroom observation, guidelines about feedback and the way in which it fits into review arrangements.
Reviewing performance	This will involve: ■ discussing preparations for the performance review including self-review by the teacher: research indicates that the more active a teacher is and the more influence s/he has in the performance review, the more likely it is that performance management will meet its objectives for all participants; ■ structuring the discussion to cover specific objectives, general discussion of strengths and achievements, and agreement on strategies to develop skills or techniques.

TABLE 1.1 *(cont'd)*

Sharing information about performance reviews	This will include: ■ every teacher to have a copy of his or her individual plan and review statement; ■ the head to have copies of all review statements; ■ information about professional development needs to be given to the person responsible for training and development at the school; ■ the head to report on performance management to the governing body; ■ a summary of head's review statement to be made available to the chief education officer, on request.
Linking reviews of performance to pay	This will involve using review information: ■ up to the threshold – to inform decisions about the award of double experience points for outstanding performance; ■ threshold – over time, evidence collected in performance reviews will contribute to judgements about whether teachers have met the threshold standards and can therefore cross the threshold; ■ above the threshold – to inform school decisions about the award of performance pay points to eligible teachers.
Monitoring and evaluating the policy in practice	The head will want to monitor the conduct and impact of performance management arrangements in reporting to the governing body, and to update and improve them over time.

The comparison between performance management and appraisal regulations is significant. First, the performance management cycle is annual compared to the biennial appraisal event. Second, the way appraisal was structured led to it being seen very much as a number of events leading up to the appraisal review – this, in effect, became the appraisal. Performance management by contrast is set out in the regulations as a cycle of continuous activity, summarised in the performance management document (DfES, 2000) as follows:

Performance management is an ongoing cycle, not an event. It involves three stages:

- *Planning: team leaders discuss and record priorities and objectives with each of the teachers in their team. They discuss how progress will be monitored.*
- *Monitoring: the teacher and team leader keep progress under review throughout the cycle, taking any supportive action needed.*
- *Review: the teacher and the team leader review achievements over the year and evaluate the teacher's overall performance, taking account of progress against objectives.*

Third, there is a distinct shift in emphasis from the focus of appraisal being almost entirely upon the professional development needs of the individual teacher, with targets (to use the language of the appraisal regulations) consisting virtually exclusively of professional development activities – i.e. the support needed to reach the next stage in the career of the teacher. Objectives in performance management are very different. While there is still a place for professional development activities, it is the job of performance management to define the outcomes desired from the work of the individual. The DfES document (2000) again offers useful guidance on how objectives should be set:

Agreeing objectives does not mean itemising every activity but picking out key expectations and yardsticks. Objectives will need to cover pupil progress as well as ways of developing and improving teachers' professional practice. These discussions should be set in the context of broader school plans.

And here lies one of the most controversial differences between performance management and appraisal: the phrase 'objectives will need to cover pupil progress' really encapsulates the shift from cosiness to accountability. The fundamental outcome of teaching is here clearly defined as pupil progress.

The final and highly significant change from appraisal is the expectation that the person who carries out performance management will be the teacher's line manager: 'the team leader should normally be the teacher who has the best overview of a teacher's work'. Many of us who were members of appraisal policy working parties in the early 1990s will remember the debates over who should carry out the appraisal process. In some schools it was pretty much left up to the individual teacher to choose their own appraiser. In other schools (in one of which we have personal experience) the appraisal structure was based principally upon sharing out the work and giving everyone 'a go'. This led to some spectacular nonsense, such as the head of music appraising the head of PE, for no other reason than he ought to appraise someone! Under performance management we move to clarity of purpose: it is about managing the performance of individual teachers and their accountability to their line manager.

Performance management provides an entirely new dialogue between teachers. It moves us on from cosy discussions between fellow professionals and into a clearer and more sharply defined relationship of line manager and line-managed. Or at least this is the theory – the difficulties arise when putting performance management into effect. Simply creating a new framework will not necessarily mean that teachers adopt the new role implied by performance management. For what we are talking about here is a complete change in the leadership and management culture of the school.

Performance management for support staff

From September 2003 teachers had new contracts that spelt out a specific set of tasks they were no longer supposed to carry out. The full list from the National Agreement *Raising Standards and Tackling Workload* is as follows:

- collecting money
- chasing absences
- bulk photocopying
- copy typing
- producing standard letters
- producing class lists
- record keeping and filing
- classroom display
- analysing attendance figures
- processing exam results
- collating pupil reports
- administering work experience
- administering examinations

- invigilating examinations
- administering teacher cover
- ICT troubleshooting and minor repairs
- commissioning new ICT equipment
- ordering supplies and equipment
- stocktaking
- cataloguing, preparing, issuing and maintaining equipment and materials
- minuting meetings
- coordinating and submitting bids
- seeking and giving personnel advice
- managing pupil data
- inputting pupil data.

This list is, by now, well known and it is perfectly clear that most of these are uncontroversial tasks and had not formed part of most teachers' duties (at least in secondary schools) for a long time, if ever. But tucked away within the list are some tasks that exemplify the very radical change in culture the new contract has ushered in for schools. Tasks such as administering examinations and teacher cover, invigilating exams and class-room display were generally carried out by teachers in most schools until quite recently, and indeed still are carried out by teachers in many schools to this day. More controversially still, the limit on teacher cover and, for primary schools in particular, the introduction of a guaranteed 10 per cent timetabled time for planning, preparation and assessment (PPA), has meant that it is now the expectation that whole classes are supervised by those other than teachers. The school workforce is going through a radical change that requires cultural change on a far greater scale than that already implied by the discussion on performance management above.

Traditionally there has been a propensity for school leadership to over-look the management and development needs of the support staff in schools. If this ever was an option, with a remodelled workforce it most certainly is not now. Typically, a remodelled school may spend a quarter or even a third of its staffing budget on support staff. With this kind of resource then, just as with the teaching workforce, leaders and managers must make sure they secure the highest levels of performance and the maximum value for money from this investment in staff. Just in the same way as for the teacher workforce, support staff need to work consistently within teams; they need to be proactively managed; they have a right to have their performance reviewed and to be given development opportunities to improve their performance at their current job; and they need career development opportunities for the future. Indeed this last point is something that may not have been considered at all until recently. For the first time we have people coming for interview for support staff posts at our schools with a view to progressing their career within this field. There are increasingly career routes for support staff and we actively need to ensure that there are more career routes in future.

Performance management for support staff has a critical place in the future of workforce development in schools.

A new school culture

A new culture is already present to a greater or lesser extent in all schools, but we believe that in all schools there is yet more to do. Schools of the future will comprise a range of experts carrying out their differing roles. The experts – the teachers – will be organised into teams led by teacher team leaders, who are the experts on teaching and learning in their team. They have the expertise, training and experience to lead teaching and learning, and see this as part of their core role. Contrast this with the old view of the head of department (or deputy head, or even headteacher) who saw their primary role as that of teacher, with any 'administrative functions' very much taking second place. Teacher team leaders need to know they have a dual role, with each as important as the other. Their contracts show that they are entitled to dedicated management time, while they are paid additional money for the teaching and learning responsibility (TLR allowances).

As a teacher, a teacher team leader is an expert practitioner; as a team leader they are accountable for the performance of their team and as such monitor the teacher in the team on a regular basis, providing teachers with frank feedback on strengths and areas for improvement. Across the team the team leader is responsible for ensuring consistent practice of the highest quality and is directive about achieving this. This consistent practice will be at all levels of activity, from basic classroom procedures, to assessment practice, to shared planning and understanding of how the subject is to be taught.

To fulfil this role the teacher team leader needs to keep in close touch with the practice of their team. But more importantly they need to be able to make judgements about performance and to be assertive about delivering these judgements to their team in order to secure the improvements in performance of their team. Improvement is achieved through the performance management procedures in the school. It is clear then that performance management is not a bolt-on extra, as may easily be implied by a minimalist approach to the framework for performance management for teachers. It is a root and branch approach that ensures high and consistent standards throughout the school.

More broadly, all team leaders in the school need to be clear about what constitutes the accepted standard of work within their team – whether this is a subject department, a year team, a key stage group, a team of IT technicians, administrators, lab technicians or whatever. In each team there needs to be a shared understanding of the work that is the team's responsibility and the standard to which it is expected to be completed. To achieve this, induction and training need to be much more rigorous, with an assessment point at the end. We believe this is an essential development – that all new employees of the school have the right to a clear understanding of what is expected of them and they have the right to be trained and developed in order to reach this standard. The implication for team leaders is clear: they need to have a thorough understanding of good practice and must be able to assess team members' ability to meet the standard. Contrast this with the situation that too often pertains in schools today: new staff join the school and are more or less expected to know what to do, or, if they don't, are left to find out for themselves. This is perhaps unfair on all those schools that do have thorough induction programmes, but even then many induction programmes simply give the briefest overview on matters such as health and safety, writing reports, how we operate our parents' evening and so on, without really ever getting near the heart of the competencies required to do the core job. Too often the assumption is that this is something the member of staff already knows. Perhaps they do, but is this really something to be taken for granted?

In short, the new culture required of schools is one where team leaders are leaders of their teams: they expect to know what is going on within their teams and expect to be accountable for the team performance.

Making it work

The performance management framework makes it clear that we have moved on from the days of the 'one-off' appraisal event – performance management is a continuous process. However, is it possible that this new process could be subverted into appraisal mark 2? Are we simply talking about an annual review of performance instead of a biennial review? How to embed the new expectations into the way the school works is the main emphasis of this book, but we need to start off from a position of understanding that it is important to have an ongoing system of management of performance of the people who work in our schools. Our proposition is that a high profile of management of performance ensures that the school runs well and achieves its goals, not only because of the higher level of control implicit in the performance management framework (and this is something that we think must be recognised), but also because it taps into the fundamental motivations of people who work in organisations.

The most basic and probably most well-known theory of human motivation is Maslow's (1987) hierarchy of needs. The famous pyramid representation of the hierarchy is shown in Fig. 1.1. The critical factor here is that motivation is a hierarchical concept, that as one satisfies lower-order needs, for example for safety and security, then it is possible to start considering the higher level need for a sense of belonging. However, if a person's physiological needs for food and water are not met they will risk their physical safety in order to meet the need for food or water. Hence the safety need is less important and can be sacrificed. Fortunately, for the most part we do not find ourselves faced with that particular dilemma and so we can concentrate on the higher orders of the motivational

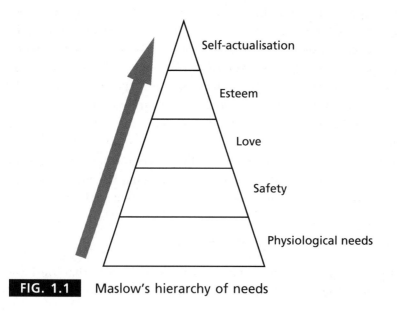

Self-actualisation

Esteem

Love

Safety

Physiological needs

FIG. 1.1   Maslow's hierarchy of needs

pyramid. A further development on this is the notion of satisfiers and dissatisfiers: the lower levels of the pyramid are required in order to gain motivation at the higher levels, but once the need is satisfied then further provision does not produce higher motivation.

Hertzberg (1966) developed this idea further in his 'motivation-hygiene theory'. He described the extent to which maintenance factors, such as food, shelter, money, etc., and self-actualisation factors, such as achievement, responsibility and recognition, act upon individual motivation. His contention was that maintenance factors, once satisfied, provide no motivation to work. It is only in their absence that they become important. Hence if a job does not pay enough to provide a worker with food or shelter then the lack of pay will be a strongly demotivating factor. Conversely if a worker has sufficient food and shelter s/he is unlikely to be motivated by the thought of more of these maintenance factors. These basic needs are unipolar variables. A similar case is made for self-actualisation factors. Thus they provide additional motivation, but their absence is not particularly demotivating (a somewhat dubious claim). Hertzberg coined the term hygiene factors for these job dissatisfiers, claiming that people need to work in a hygienic environment, i.e. one where job dissatisfiers have been removed.

As our performance management systems are all rooted in the notion of creating higher-performing schools through higher-performing employees then we need to understand the different ways in which the process can tap into these motivations. Clearly, performance management is dealing with the upper echelons of any motivational hierarchy. But even within this there are different approaches depending upon how much an individual's motivational needs are already being met. There is all the difference in the world between performance management of a younger, highly ambitious teacher who sees their future in senior school leadership, and the same process applied to, for example, the school bursar who might well be a grandmother and nearing retirement. In the first case the appeal is to the lower levels of Maslow's hierarchy. It is likely that money is a significant motivator for such a person, as they may be struggling with financial security – perhaps having young children that present a fearsome drain on household income. Such an ambitious individual is likely to have high levels of need for recognition and self-esteem, and so the process can easily tap into all of these motivations.

Contrast this with the second case of the school bursar nearing retirement. Here, it is highly likely that all the lower-level needs are satisfied to a high degree. This person is probably financially stable and has all the recognition and self-esteem they need coming from outside the workplace. Performance management only really has the self-actualisation motive to tap into. Too often it is tempting to dismiss the needs of colleagues such as this, but we need to remember that simply being at work is fulfilling some purpose and this is most likely related to self-actualisation. If we are to performance manage successfully under such circumstances then recognition of this very important higher-order motivation is critical in order to gain the most from this employee.

As well as understanding the motivations of those whom we line manage, we must also understand ourselves and how we look at the world. What is our own analysis of the motivations of other people, and how can we gain the best from our teams? Douglas McGregor (1960) provides a simple theory to analyse the paradigm a manager operates within. He identified two poles of a continuum – theory X and theory Y:

- *Theory X.* Managers who operate according to theory X believe that people are essentially lazy and will do the minimum they can get away with. The only way to ensure people do their work is to monitor them carefully, to incentivise them through means such as performance-related pay and to punish them when things go wrong or when work is not complete.

- *Theory Y.* This is the polar opposite of theory X. These managers believe that people inherently wish to do a good job at work. Left to their own devices, people will produce the goods. This paradigm places a low emphasis upon monitoring, rewards and sanction, and a high level of emphasis upon team building, development opportunities and the like.

Understanding where you stand in this spectrum – and also understanding the motivation theories outlined previously – should provide the foundations for a strong and useful performance management process that will create the conditions for each member of staff to improve their performance.

_____ Conclusion _____

In this chapter we have identified the way in which the culture in schools has shifted over recent years. As long ago as 1976 James Callaghan famously raised the issue of the 'secret garden' of schooling in his Ruskin College speech. At this time the notion of teacher professionalism – the teacher as master/mistress of their own classroom and all that went on within it, and the teacher being responsible for the curriculum taught and the ways and means of most effectively teaching it – was at its high water mark. At that time the very idea that one teacher would observe the teaching of another and make judgements upon it was a complete anathema; still less that there should be any notion of common purpose between teachers within the same school (or even the same department). Those days cast a long shadow, and throwbacks can still be discerned in some schools and in conversations with teachers who cut their teeth at that time and have not found the times that followed entirely to their liking.

Our contention is that the professionalism described above is a false professionalism – perhaps it is indicative of a professional notion of the individual, but it does not result in a professional organisation. Contrast this with the modern school. Here teachers work in teams under the leadership of a head of department or otherwise entitled team leader. There is an expectation that the team leader will lead and manage their team and that collectively they will develop consistent good practice within their department. These teams are collected under the leadership of the headteacher and leadership team, who perform the same function across the school. Teachers are provided with the support they need and the resource backup to effect the outcomes they desire. All this takes place within a context where team leaders expect to manage the performance of their teams and provide them with feedback and development to ensure that they can achieve the institutional goals. This is a truly professional approach, ensuring schools provide the service for which they are created.

References

Barlett, S. (1998) 'Teacher perceptions of the purposes of staff appraisal: a response to Kyriacou' *Teacher Development*, vol. 2, no. 3, University of Wolverhampton.

Bennett, H. (1999) 'One drop of blood: teacher appraisal mark 2' *Teacher Development*, vol. 3, no. 3, Leeds Metropolitan University.

Callaghan, J. (1976) Ruskin College speech, 18 October 1976, in Moon, B., Murphy, P. and Raynor, J. (eds) (1989) *Policies for the Curriculum*, The Open University, Hodder & Stoughton, London.

DfES (2000) *Performance Management in Schools*, 0051/2000, London.

Hertzberg, F. (1966) *Work and the Nature of Man*, World Publishing, New York.

Maslow, A. (1987) *Motivation and Personality*, 3rd edition, HarperCollins, London.

McGregor, D. (1960) *The Human Side of Enterprise*, McGraw-Hill, New York.

chapter two

Creating the policy

Creating a policy

Elements of the policy

Lesson observation

Other staff and workforce reform

Conclusion

It is worth spending a few moments thinking about why we have policies at all. Why do we need a policy on anything and what happens if we don't? Why does it matter? In particular, why do organisations need policies? Think about a school where there is no policy on anything. In this school, teachers will teach what they like to students who do as they like. Everyone will do as they please, wear what they please and achieve as they please. Does this sound like an organisation? By looking at other organisations and structures we get a sense of what it means. One of the more complex and complicated organisations is the health service. Like many publicly funded structures it has to serve an increasingly demanding population (with expectations of what medicine can do to improve, transform and indeed save lives) and has to deliver an improved and continuously improving service (because the relationship between the patient and doctor is being transformed into a client one). Of course, more is expected from the resources applied to the service (because while in real and relative terms the amount of money applied to the service may have increased considerably, so too have the demands made on the service as more is being asked when more is applied). Looking at the way the health service chooses to manage these conflicting and demanding issues gives us a valuable insight into the need for the organisation and the policies that we can choose to achieve organisational goals.

The Department for Health has an organisation policy that determines how all areas of the NHS and social care are structured, financed and managed. Specifically it has policies in the following areas:

- *Modernisation.* The organisational structure of the NHS is being renewed so that it can respond better to the priorities of local patients and frontline staff, with a plan to show how it will be able to respond to the needs of patients and other stakeholders. Notice the reference is also to frontline staff. If we apply this to the school context the plan is very much about addressing the needs of the children and the local community as well as the needs of the teachers and support staff.

- *Finance and planning.* In this section there is a detailed guide to NHS planning, spending and income. The Department provides specific guidance to hospitals and other service providers about financial reforms and processes, fund and grant allocation, direct payments and the planning framework. This is a policy on how the finance and the planning mechanism will work. Again, apply this to the school context and we have a need for finance and planning mechanism that supports the implementation of the plans that are designed to address the needs of children.

- *Primary care.* The Department has policies, plans and initiatives to improve the organisation of primary care in England. Areas covered include investment plans, primary care workforce development, the use of information technology and the administrative structure and roles of different types of primary care trusts. In the school context this is the planning that goes into the work in classrooms.

- *Secondary care.* The Department has policies, plans and initiatives to improve the organisation of secondary care in England. These include new ways of providing secondary care (for example, treatment centres), the programme to give all patients access to pre-booked appointments at a time of their choice, and guidance about hospital management and development. In the school context this is the planning that goes into the work that supports children in classrooms (perhaps the education psychology service, education social work and so on).

- *Integrated care.* Policies, plans and initiatives to improve the organisation of integrated care in England include care trusts, programmes to make hospital admission and discharge more efficient, and financial arrangements to support users and providers of long-term or residential care. In the school context this is the planning to make sure that department structures integrate well – that there is curriculum planning across the school and also that there is effective and efficient interdepartment and interdisciplinary provision.

There are also policies on emergency care, records management, patient and public involvement, complaints, social services performance assessment, commissioning, health and safety and self-care. It is only a small step from public health policy that is applied to the work of health-care providers to the daily work of nurses, doctors and other health professionals.

By extrapolating these ideas across to the education context we get a flavour of the need for policy development because the policies articulate what we want and what we are going to do. Moreover, they articulate what is going to happen to those who are involved in the organisation. Read the policy on emergency care and it is possible to work out what will happen to us when taken seriously ill or are involved in a medical emergency. Read the policy on self-care and we can see what kind of provision we will have to make for ourselves, and what level of provision will be made for us. Apply this to schools and policy development and we have not only a statement of intention but also a clear idea of what we want and what we are going to do. Of course this is sustained by the legal framework in which schools operate. For example, new appraisal regulations came into force in September 2001, which were a consolidation of the 2000 regulations. The governing body is responsible for establishing the school's performance management policy, with reference to the DfES Model Performance Management Policy (www.teachernet. gov.uk/_doc/5175/model_policy.doc).

This chapter is about formulating a performance management policy for a school (which will address the needs of both teachers and support staff). The performance management of teachers is statutory and is subject to the legal framework. As such there is no discretion – teachers have to be appraised as part of the policy implementation. In addition, the performance management process must include a lesson observation, and the objectives set must include one that relates to pupil progress. There is no discretion over this. However, there is considerable discretion over much that accompanies the performance management system, or to give it another name, the appraisal system. And whether we choose to call it performance management or appraisal is in many ways an important decision. Appraisal has notions of classification according to worth, based perhaps on some analysis or evaluation. Performance management is a process that is ongoing. It will have summative points but is not something that happens once a year. Instead, it is part of a construct where the work of each member of the organisation is subject to continuous appraisal based on the principle of people continually improving.

The principles of effective performance management lie in three main areas:

- *Aims of the school.* The aims of the school should be concordant with the principles of the performance management system. The aims of the school should be to develop all staff, improve the quality of teaching and raise standards of achievement for all children – hopefully the latter statements form part of the aims or mission statement for the school. The process to achieve these aims has to be through appropriate and effective professional development in a supportive manner – in the same way that the potential of the children or students is realised through the high-quality teaching and learning environment. Thus the aims of the school will set out what the school seeks to achieve for the children of the school community, often with some kind of supporting statement that explains how this potential will be realised. The aims of the performance management policy should reflect or mirror these whole school aims.

■ *Policy of performance management*. As was discussed earlier, the policy is the articulation of the school's aims, setting down what is going to happen and why it is important. It also involves the who, the what, the why and how – although the fact that the policy exists at all shows that the performance of the staff in the school matters.

■ *Techniques and skills for effective development*. The way that the policy is implemented is key to its success. We believe that where meetings are arranged then there will be progress. The simple act of requiring two people – where one is the superordinate and the other the subordinate – to meet regularly is in itself a good place to start. If people are required to meet once every six weeks then they will have to talk about something! However, turning this rather nebulous discussion into a focused appraisal of the individual's performance requires something more.

Creating a policy

Performance management can be hugely problematic in schools. Teachers can be very wary of making judgements of one another and therefore a process that routinely requires them to consider the performance of others can be fraught with danger. However, many schools have made much progress defining the layers of accountability in the school. Target setting has indeed sharpened this particular saw. Broadly, the principle is that while the headteacher is responsible for the performance of the school, the heads of department are responsible for the performance of the department and class teachers are responsible for the performance of their classes. This all sounds very straightforward, but because of the emphasis on the attainment of children there are also many other dimensions to the performance of a teacher, head of department, school leader or headteacher. In addition, we need to consider those whose performance cannot be measured through pupil progress – for example, support staff working in the general office. While the principles of performance management apply equally to each member of staff in the school, the way in which the performance is managed and assessed varies a good deal.

So, we need a process that is not simply a blunt instrument that sets pupil performance targets and measures the individual against those targets, but rather one that encompasses a range of dimensions. There are a number of ways in which these can be articulated (for example, the National Standards, Hay McBer competencies and so on). In our view, the threshold standards provide a useful benchmark and also a useful framework for discussion. These are as follows:

- knowledge and understanding;
- teaching and assessment – planning lessons;
- teaching and assessment – classroom management;
- teaching and assessment – monitoring progress;
- pupil progress;
- wider professional effectiveness – personal development;
- wider professional effectiveness – school development;
- professional characteristics.

(The application form for performance threshold standards assessment can be found at www.teachernet.gov.uk/_doc/7321/taaf.doc, which has links to the criteria for each standard.)

We believe that schools should set up a working group to consider all these issues and decide how they want to phrase the policy.

Setting up a working group

A working group is an effective way to develop school policy because it enables the school to harness the best practice and coordinate the efforts of groups. Where there is no policy then groups of teachers can discuss their practice, albeit in an informal way. Some departments and teams will have existing methods and protocols for working together. Setting up a working group gives space for this good practice to be voiced and policy can be built up from this point.

Performance management is statutory and it is the responsibility of the governors that such a policy exists. Therefore the working group might include:

- representatives from the governors;
- heads of department and heads of year;
- union or professional association representatives;
- main scale teachers;
- leadership team representation.

It is our advice that a member of the leadership team should chair the working group but that the head should not be involved. The head should review the policy before it is presented to the staff and the governors for approval.

_____ Elements of the policy _____

The following section outlines the main elements of the policy to be developed by the working group.

Introduction

Sometimes people benefit from having a statement that sets out why there is a need for a performance management policy. The most obvious statement is that it is statutory and the school is required by law to have a policy. In some schools this might be considered sufficient but it is an opportunity to articulate some of the key principles by relating the policy to the aims of the school.

Rationale

Again, this element should not be too problematic. The rationale is that the school is required to have a performance management policy, but at this point we move into the discussion of what the policy of performance management seeks to achieve.

CASE STUDY 1

Agreeing the rationale

Hammer School already has a performance management system. Each year there is a discussion between the nominated person and the teacher about their work. This year, for example, the head of PE reviewed the work of the head of history. The head of history was supposed to write up his review meeting, but six months later it hasn't happened.

Kate had been asked by the headteacher to chair the working group on performance management. At the first meeting Kate was leading a discussion on the policy and found herself in the middle of a heated discussion between a union representative and a community governor. The community governor asserted that in his company performance management was a good way to decide who received pay awards and that the school should have this as part of the policy. In his view the rationale was to implement a pay policy. The union representative hotly disagreed and said that performance management was to make sure that staff doing a very difficult job felt valued and that their training needs were identified.

The case study illustrates the importance of a working group. There is clearly a range of opinions on the purposes of the policy and the working group gives the stakeholders the opportunity to air these and for them to be discussed and resolved. For the chair of the group, Kate, the important steps to take in managing this situation are as follows:

- Establish with the headteacher the remit of the group. The two people have to be clear on the purpose of the group and the scope of the group. In most cases there is a need for a policy (because the school has a statutory responsibility to have one) and so the group is there to create a draft policy that will go out for consultation to members of staff before it is presented to the governors for consideration and adoption.

- Identify the role of the members of the group. The choice of membership is very important to the way the group will work. Governors who have some expertise in this area are very useful – for example, if they have a background in the law it is very handy to have immediate clarification on legal principles or the minutiae of employment law. However, they will need to be briefed, ideally by the headteacher, to ensure that they understand what the purpose of the policy is. For a governor to respond in the way presented in the case study is likely to rile union representatives because performance management has always needed to be separated from decisions on pay, in the same way that it is separated from competency procedures. Of course, progression on the upper pay spine has complicated matters in that it is conditional on sustained high performance, and indeed threshold assessment is contingent on evidence from performance reviews, but the link should never be explicit between performance review and pay. Union representatives are included in the group because the policy affects their members and the way in which conditions of service are implemented. Although not essential to the working group, we strongly advise union representation on matters concerning pay, conditions of service, performance and the like. However, by inviting union representatives to be part of such a group means that the chair is discussing conditions of service with the unions, so it is vital that Kate approaches the meetings with care, chooses her words carefully and makes sure she is well briefed on the law.

■ Set out a timetable and an agenda for the meetings. It is good practice to set out the timetable for the meetings stating when and where the meetings will take place and the provisional outcomes from each. This will focus the attention of the group and also emphasise the need for members of the group to do some preparation in anticipation of the meetings. Having a timescale for the production of the draft policy, consultation and eventual conclusion to work of the group does focus the efforts of the members. Again, compiling minutes in the form of sections of the policy is good practice because it sustains the momentum of the working group and means that the outcomes of the meeting are kept high on the agenda.

■ Set up individual and bilateral meetings. It can be useful to have bilateral discussions with individuals or groups between meetings. So one outcome from this difficult meeting would be for Kate to have an individual discussion with the governor and with the union representative. Sometimes asking them to find a form of words to explain their point of view, as part of the policy, is a good way forward. This gives everyone the opportunity to reflect on the situation.

The most important thing for Kate, however, is to do her homework and be clear on the principles so that the policy development does not get sidetracked by arguments that can be easily resolved by reference to the law.

Roles

The purpose of this section is to introduce the roles of different people in the performance management process. The system operated by Hammer School in the case study is one where there is a discussion and the teacher writes up their own review statement. At the working group it has been agreed that a broader definition of performance management needs to be considered and that the system needs to incorporate the totality of the work that goes on during the year.

CASE STUDY 2

Agreeing aims and roles

Hammer School's working group agree the following aims of the performance management system.

Evaluation goals:

- To give feedback to staff so that they are clear about their current level of performance.
- To develop a valid basis on which progression can be determined.
- To provide a means for identifying unsatisfactory performance.

Development goals:

- To counsel and coach staff so that they can improve their performance and develop future potential.
- To develop commitment to the organisation through discussion of career opportunities and career planning.
- To motivate staff through recognition of achievement and support.
- To strengthen relationships.
- To identify and diagnose individual and organisational problems.

Individual goals:

- To receive feedback on performance and progress.
- To discuss present roles and amend the job description if changes are agreed.
- To identify opportunities for personal professional development.
- To identify training opportunities.
- To discuss aspirations and career plans.

The question of professional judgement is discussed in the working group meeting and some express concern on how they will gather evidence and make informed judgements – some of the group are very unhappy about the principle of making judgements about their colleagues.

Again, the case study underlines the importance of having a working group because the group allows space for concerns to be expressed openly. In this case the issues are reasonably clear: the responsibility for the performance of a teacher rests with the line manager. The line manager is accountable for the results and the outcomes of their area. However, there will be some colleagues who express misgivings and reservations about the sanctity of the classroom and will be wary of making judgements (often because they don't want others to judge them). These are very important issues and a strong lead has to be articulated by the headteacher. To allay fears there needs to be training and development for staff, as well as review, complaint and grievance procedures in case anything goes wrong.

Responsibility for reviews

A basic question to ask is 'who is going to do the review?' Although superficially this seems obvious, it is fundamental to making the process manageable. Deciding who does the reviews is a statement of how performance management links with line management.

CASE STUDY 3

Dividing responsibilities

Hammer School's current policy is that everyone with a responsibility allowance is involved in reviewing the work of another person. The science department is the largest in the school and the team is reviewed by seven different people.

The headteacher tells Kate that the system leads to inconsistency and makes it very difficult to keep track of the process. People have commented to Kate that they find it really difficult talking to someone they don't know well about their performance and that the review meetings are often spent explaining in detail what has been done.

Kate wants to present some ideas to the working group.

This is a good example of where some market research is useful. Finding out from people about their experience of performance management and what they would like from the process is a good way forward. One scenario would be to continue the existing arrangements but provide additional training for staff. Another would be to align the performance management arrangements to the line management of the school. However, this may mean that some people will have a large number of people to appraise. For example, the head of science in the case study would be responsible for the performance management of the science team. Of course, some of this responsibility could be delegated to others (such large departments often have people who hold positions of responsibility). The benefit of this approach is that the link between day-to-day management and performance management is explicit and there is a consistency of approach across a team. So although there may be issues that arise from having the head of history reviewing the work of all the history teachers, at least the issues are located in one area and can be tackled in a systematic and focused manner.

Presenting the working group with a range of possible ways forward is an effective way of managing a working party. It enables people to consider the issues fully and think about the needs of the wider staff team rather than focusing on 'what it means for me'.

Thinking about the timing is the next section of the policy.

Timing of reviews

When a review happens is just as important as what happens and how it happens. Thinking about the timing of the process – setting objectives, planning, monitoring and reviewing – is crucial to the performance management process.

Most teachers start work in schools at the beginning of the academic year and so their induction year runs from September to August. The outcome of this induction year is normally success and so it is good practice for teachers commencing their second year of teaching to have development targets for this new phase of their career. As such, a cycle of review that runs in parallel with the school year makes sense. In addition, there is a statutory requirement that all teachers have their pay formally reviewed by the governing body annually. Normally the headteacher advises on progression (it is unusual for an increment on the main professional scale to be withheld) on the scale, and this is also the case for the leadership team. Therefore, timing formal reviews at the end of the school academic year makes sense because they provide an evidence base for this pay process.

One drawback is that having a review in June or July means that the outcomes cannot be judged against pupil performance where these rely on key stage results. This is a major disadvantage because the process that underpins performance management should impact on pupil performance – hence the statutory requirement that one objective should relate to pupil progress. However, timing the reviews at the beginning of the school year might mean that some teachers do not have a review of their objectives because they have moved schools at the end of the previous academic year.

Timing the process is thus a difficult decision and there will inevitably be compromises. In some local authorities the statutory target setting occurs late in the autumn term and so the link between statutory target setting and the headteachers' targets is difficult to sustain – the effect of aligning these two is to push the review of the teaching staff into the spring term. The benefit of this is that the review falls part-way through the school year and enables progress to be considered in the light of whole-school progress, departmental progress and the implementation of the development plan.

Performance management cycle

Having decided on the timing it is then necessary to work out the performance management cycle – how objectives will be determined, and how they will be monitored and reviewed over time.

A critical aspect to performance management is the link between the individual's performance and that of the whole organisation. Simply put, the school's performance is made up of department performances which, in turn, are made up of teacher performances – and of course, all of these depend on the efforts of each student at the school. Bringing all these aspects together to form a coherent system that links student and teacher performance is tricky. There is already a link between performance and pay – not in the industrial sense where increased production and performance lead to increased pay, but in the sense that threshold assessment and progression, on the upper pay spine at least, depend on high levels of performance. But what happens if a teacher does not meet their performance objectives – what happens if the pupil performance target is missed?

CASE STUDY 4

Agreeing performance objectives

Hammer School's working group on performance management has agreed the principles for the policy and is clear on why it is important. It has agreed that the performance reviews are the responsibility of the line manager, since this will bring about a coherence in the structure. It is happy that the line manager should also conduct the performance review.

Kate now wants the group to consider the pupil progress objectives. Hammer School is a high performing one but analysis suggests that value-added is weak.

One of the governors works for a large credit card company; his company has three categories of performance objectives that he thinks could be transferred to Hammer School:

- *Floor*. This is the target that includes no value-added. For subjects at GCSE it might be determined by cognitive ability tests or progress charts produced by the DfES.

- *Challenge*. This is the target where current performance is measured against predictions based on some notions of value-added. If cognitive ability data were used, it might be an average of 0.5 of a grade above expectation.

- *Stretch*. This would be an exceptional result. The concept of the challenge target might be to improve significantly the results in a school with high levels of value-added.

This governor is keen to introduce the principle of these categories of targets into the performance management process at Hammer School. Kate isn't sure – is the school ready and how will teachers react?

The case study demonstrates once again the benefits of having the working group. The group allows the flow of ideas – for new challenges to be put forward and discussed. So a working group needs to be structured to encourage freedom of expression and a willingness to contribute and engage in debate.

Whether the school decides to have targets expressed in this way is less relevant than showing what targets will mean to the teaching staff. One way to progress this discussion is to prepare targets for a specimen group. So a particular department and group of teachers could identify the grades that students would have to achieve in order for the performance to meet the floor, challenge and stretch principles. Making the process concrete – saying to people that this is what it would mean for you, your class, and your colleagues – is an effective way to broker a discussion.

An issue that might be raised at this point is what happens if people achieve the stretch target or the challenge target, or, indeed, fail to meet the floor target? The link between review and pay cannot be introduced at this point – to do so risks difficulties with the unions, and of course exposes the school to a financial liability (if everyone meets their challenge targets and if the policy states a bonus or pay rise, then what happens if the school cannot pay this?). People will worry about what happens if they don't meet the floor targets, while others may feel that by not meeting (or indeed exceeding) the stretch target that they, too, will have failed. Having a process where people agree to targets is therefore fundamental and by linking the performance management policy to the target-setting system the link is implicit but not explicit. The necessary separation is preserved.

Links between pay, career stages and performance management

This section of the policy is important to clarify the link between the performance management system and other policies (such as threshold assessment and upper pay spine progression). We suggested earlier in the chapter that performance review be carried out under the headings for threshold assessment (see page 22). Of course the school may want to raise a whole range of other issues (for example, using the National Standards for subject leaders or any of the other standards or competency models). These can be covered amply under the heading of professional characteristics. The benefit of using the threshold standards (as well as aiding tracking for progression) is that there is a clear distinction between the work of a subject leader as a classroom teacher and as a team leader. Using the National Standards for headteachers as the headings for the leadership team may be fine but may neglect the classroom teacher role that fills a good portion of many leadership team members.

In summary, performance management needs to include a review of progress but also needs to guide people and be the mechanism for identifying development areas and prioritising training needs.

Managing weak performance

This section of the policy explains that the performance management process does not form part of any formal disciplinary or capability processes but may inform certain decisions or recommendations.

Confidentiality

The policy must emphasise the confidential nature of performance management documents and the need to keep them in a secure place. There needs to be a mechanism for review documents to be handed in, read and filed. The review is a confidential document between the reviewer and the teacher and the headteacher. As such, arrangements need to be in place to ensure that review documents are secure. All schools should have secure places where personnel records are kept. This may be difficult when security hinges on the headteacher checking if things have been done – in a large school this can be especially problematic.

One answer is to have a coversheet for performance reviews. This states the name of the teacher, the name of the reviewer and the date. There is a tick box to confirm that the pack includes a lesson observation, a review of the previous objectives and new objectives for the year ahead. The pack is passed to the headteacher's PA who checks them off on a list and places them in the headteacher's tray. This means that the PA can manage the receipt of the documents and do the necessary chasing up without confidentiality being compromised.

Access to outcomes

The policy should outline the statutory position about who can have access to review statements or information contained in them. This is covered in the above section.

Complaints

The policy must set out the statutory process to follow if a complaint is made about the annual review.

CASE STUDY 5

Airing grievances

The working group at Hammer School has made progress and has agreed the principles of the performance management system. It has agreed that there will be a termly meeting between each teacher and the line manager specifically to review progress. The reviews will be carried out once a year, using the threshold standards. Alison, the head of geography, goes to see Kate just before the last meeting to say that she is concerned about what will happen when her review is carried out by the assistant head. Alison and the assistant head (who was previously head of geography at the school) have never really 'seen eye to eye' and there have been several instances where heated discussion has taken place. Alison has had to work hard to move the department from being a solid but staid performer. This has involved introducing ICT into classes and using this instead of textbooks. The assistant head is known to disapprove of this development.

Alison is an ambitious teacher who is keen to succeed to leadership team level and has her threshold assessment this year. How might Kate respond to Alison?

As the case study demonstrates, the issue of what happens when people don't get on is an important one to air. If performance management is to be beneficial and contribute to school improvement then it needs to be part of a system that challenges and supports teachers and, indeed, other staff. If it is to challenge and support people then it has to be prepared to offer criticism and guide people through to new solutions. This is the subject of much of the discussion in Chapter 3. In many ways there is very little that Kate can say to reassure Alison except that all the statements will be reviewed by the headteacher and that there is a complaints procedure (which is a statutory element of the policy) and that she will be entitled to air her grievance in this forum. Of course, Alison's reaction might be that she doesn't want to take out a grievance, and then Kate's advice has to be that Alison is able to raise concerns informally with the headteacher. Kate might challenge Alison further by saying that if she is not prepared to raise an issue formally, then how much of an issue is it? Although that is a somewhat harsh way of tackling the issue with Alison, it is an important part of engaging in professional dialogue about performance.

Evaluation of the policy

Finally, the policy emphasises the school's commitment to review the effectiveness of the review process each year.

Completing the process

By forming a working group to draw up a policy of performance management there is a clear understanding at all levels of what it entails. By the end of the process there should be a policy that says the following:

- what will happen to people;
- when it will happen;
- who will be involved;
- how it will be recorded;

- how the objectives will be reviewed and set for the following period;
- what the outcomes of the process are and what rights people have if things go wrong.

_____ Lesson observation _____

One element of the process for teachers is the lesson observation. Decisions need to be taken about how the lesson observation fits into the whole performance management process. It seems to us nonsense that a teacher is only observed by their line manager as part of a professional review. It is, in our view, only through a focus on teaching and learning that teachers improve their practice. It is only by teachers improving their practice that schools improve. Improvement all comes down to what goes on in our classrooms.

There is widespread variance in lesson observation. One school known to us has atomised the teaching process to a set of statements. These include 'register is taken at the start of the lesson', 'there is a seating plan' and so on. We believe that the richness of the teaching process cannot be atomised in this way. There is a place for being able to assess the extent to which school policies are being implemented (for example, the register at the beginning of each lesson), but breaking it down into a tickbox model seems to be at odds with, for example, the Ofsted criteria for excellence, which states that 'Difficult ideas or skills are taught in an inspiring and highly effective way.' We think the way to teaching excellence is through professional dialogue and the sharing of good practice. The first step is, therefore, to agree on some measure or standard of teaching quality that can be used consistently across the school.

This can be achieved by using the Ofsted framework. There are drawbacks to the framework (in that it does not, for example, allow for thematic monitoring) but the big advantage is that it links clearly with Ofsted and the criteria are reasonably straightforward to apply. However, if this framework is going to be used effectively then all the staff involved in lesson observation will need to be trained to use the framework and to give feedback.

Having arranged for training, the next question is how to deal with all the information. First, how will the information be collected? Teachers must be observed and a report compiled using the framework as part of the performance review. As we stated earlier, it is a nonsense to confine lesson observations to once a year: there needs to be regular, informed discussion about the quality of teaching in the school. One way is to ask all team leaders to set out a calendar of lesson observations in their department for the whole academic year, with the baseline expectation that each teacher will be observed at least twice per year and that newly qualified teachers will be observed once per half term. This is the minimum level of activity. For a department of, for example, six teachers this adds up to at least twelve observations. From this it is possible to draw conclusions about the quality of teaching in the department. The leadership team can collect all these lesson observations (for a staff of 60 this means 120 observations per year) and so begin to create a picture of the teaching quality and analyse the main issues. Collecting the lesson reports is made easier by the calendar – a requirement that the lesson reports go into an individual's file is a useful strategy to ensure that people pass them on. If the lesson reports are not forthcoming, then perhaps a more rigorous collection system needs to be developed.

Second, the information must be analysed. The point about lesson observations is that they are developmental for the teacher being observed and to some extent to the person observing. The act of giving feedback strengthens the role of the team leader – and having a professional discussion about teaching quality and strategy is the sign of a healthy school. A structure that asks the team leader to analyse the themes that emerge from the lesson observations and feed these into the development plan is an effective way to embed lesson observations into the process. Themes that emerge from the analysis of the whole staff can feed into the development plan and influence the INSET day programme.

Other staff and workforce reform

In the early part of 2003 the DfES undertook a consultation exercise on its proposals to improve the workload of teachers and school managers. The strategies proposed were in response to a report produced by PricewaterhouseCoopers (PwC) in 2001. The PwC report identified a whole range of tasks that were routinely undertaken by teachers and school managers. Interestingly, it was secondary headteachers who had the greatest workload; anecdotally we think that this will have been some surprise to the teaching body. In fact, a survey in August 2005 (*Times Educational Supplement*, 2005) showed that secondary headteachers remained those with the greatest workload.

Teacher workload is problematic, in general terms because of the effect it has on recruitments and retention, and absence through stress and sickness. More importantly, perhaps, one of the most striking effects of teachers spending time photocopying, invigilating examinations and so on is that this is time (and consequently money) that is wasted. We listed the administrative and clerical tasks that teachers should no longer carry out in Chapter 1 (see page 8). By avoiding these tasks there may be a real opportunity to shift the emphasis, quite correctly, to teaching and learning.

Reducing workload is only half the workforce reform story; the other is very much about raising standards. There are some issues where there is no discretion – for example, staff may not undertake bulk photocopying, and if staff are freed from teaching because of a school trip then any cover they do must count towards their 38 hours of cover per year (and of course there should be pressure from schools to reduce this number of hours). However, the National Agreement (*Raising Standards and Tackling Workload*) places an onus on school leaders to rethink the way in which things are done and also gives considerable scope to do things in new ways; so if teachers cannot invigilate exams or cover for classes during gained time, then they can teach classes, produce resources and undertake a wider range of teaching and learning activities. This must be a good thing – we want our teachers to spend their time working on activities that improve the quality of teaching and learning: we want them to spend their time raising standards.

One outcome of this debate has been the increase in the number of support staff in schools and their strategic importance. Schools are employing industry-standard professionals to undertake estate management, financial planning, personnel management and secretarial functions. In many schools now the number of support staff, on a head count, equates or exceeds the number of teachers. Ask all the staff to attend a staff meeting and this quickly and visibly shows itself to be the case.

The performance of support staff has to be managed in the same way as for teachers, but it has frequently received less attention. The principles of support staff performance management are the same as for teachers but the measures we use to review their work are different – their jobs are different from those of the teaching staff. This will be discussed in detail in Chapter 6.

Conclusion

The guiding principle of this book is that all staff are entitled to know the standards expected of them and the job they are required to do, and to have their work reviewed against these two set of criteria. All staff have objectives and these should be reviewed regularly to ensure that progress is maintained and any support measures put in place where possible. Developing a robust performance management system is fundamental to school improvement. The two are not separated by principle or practice – if they are then the school has got it wrong. We start from an agreement that there is a statutory obligation to carry out performance reviews. In the case of a teacher, it must include lesson observation and a pupil performance target. The rest is up to us to decide.

Reference

Times Educational Supplement (2005) 'Still crazy after all those hours', 19 August, quoting the School Teachers Review Body.

chapter three

The coaching paradigm

Meetings

The coaching model in action

The benefits of the coaching paradigm

Conclusion

In Chapter 1 we discussed some of the history and rationale for the changes in legislation on teacher performance management, rooted as it was in the belief that the pre-existing appraisal system had become little more than a biennial cosy chat. In Chapter 2 we went on to discuss the creation of policy and ways of engaging the whole staff in the process. However, even with a legal framework and with the most engaging policy process it is by no means certain that the culture change we have discussed will simply happen. Schools can be places of tremendous inertia and resilience to change, especially when considering deep-rooted changes to how things are done, not just what is done. It is certainly possible that having gone through all the policy development the school may well end up with a situation not markedly different from the appraisal process that had been replaced.

What we need to consider is how to create a process that genuinely manages the performance of staff in school and is not simply another word for the old appraisal system. The goal is to create a system that manages performance through a suitably supportive but also sufficiently focused procedure. The approach is based very heavily upon staff development through coaching.

Meetings

This approach is heavily dependent upon one-to-one meetings. Each member of the leadership team has a team of colleagues that report to them; for example, the deputy head line-manages all the heads of department, and one of the assistant heads manages the heads of year. In turn these team members are in charge of their own teams. To support the coaching paradigm there is an absolute expectation that each team leader will meet with each team member individually on a regular basis. The frequency depends upon the size of the team and (in the case of heads of department, for example) the time available to carry out these meetings. The head meets with each member of the leadership team once a week; the assistant head meets with heads of year every two weeks; the deputy meets with heads of department every four weeks. Each teacher has an entitlement to an individual meeting of 30 minutes with their head of department each half term.

Now this lengthy description of meetings sounds like a prescription for endless meetings-bloody-meetings. How does this system, which on the face of it is the antithesis of 'modern management' with its delayering principles and empowerment models, deliver school improvement? Surely all it delivers is staff weighed down by bureaucracy? This would be a risk if the system was not based upon the school development plan and action-focused. For example, if the heads of department team are required by their development plans to work upon improving attainment at GCSE, to improve schemes of work and to improve assessment in their departments, then these items form a clear agenda for a sequence of meetings. So at an initial meeting a head of department might be asked to produce a commentary upon their most recent GCSE results. This commentary will illuminate some issues, which doubtless will include matters relating to schemes of work and assessment. Through discussion, a series of action points will emerge, which can be minuted and become actions for the next meeting. At the next meeting progress can be reviewed and new action points will emerge.

But why is there a need for the meeting – could this not all be done on paper? Certainly, progress could be recorded, action points and deadlines set, new progress recorded and so on. But this is where we come to the crux of the matter. The purpose of the meeting with a head of department is not simply a monitoring exercise (as has been described above), rather it is a coaching opportunity. The key purpose of the meeting is, in fact, staff development. In the example it may not be evident to the head of department where the issues in their department lie: it is only through skilled questioning and probing that these issues can be teased out. Perhaps the head of department has not considered schemes of work, or may indeed actively disagree with the whole concept of schemes of work (it does happen); then the meeting is an opportunity for the team leader to work through this and make the case. Again this will rely upon skilful questioning and probing, but over a relatively short period of time dramatic changes can result from this approach. Running throughout all these discussions is the alignment of culture referred to above. The outcome when this system is performed well is a cohesive team with a deep shared understanding of the expectations they should have of themselves, their team and their pupils, and also an understanding of what is expected of them.

At leadership group level it is common practice to have a weekly leadership group meeting. What place do one-to-ones have here? The answer depends very much upon the nature of the leadership group. It is our view that it is more efficient and leads to greater consistency for senior colleagues to have complete responsibility for aspects of the school; hence our somewhat traditional pastoral/curriculum divide. Accepting this to be the case then the place of the leadership group meeting becomes a discussion of items that have already been thought through. Bringing problems without suggested answers to the leadership group is wasteful of time and leads to shoddy decision making. In this structure those with responsibility for an area have the responsibility of doing the thinking on that area, preparing discussion papers for the team as appropriate. The thinking has to take place some time, and so this is one of the reasons for the weekly bilateral meeting between a team member and team leader. Broadly, the school improvement plan forms the agenda for the meeting, and the issues relating to implementation are thought through. Perhaps this will include rehearsing a particularly difficult meeting, going through a lesson observation note to arrive at a judgement, or considering what steps need to be taken with a member of staff who is underperforming. It is important that these things are gone through, not only because the team member may not know what or how to go about achieving the desired ends, but also because this provides an opportunity for *the* as opposed to *a* way to be determined. By discussing these issues the team member knows not only that they are pursuing the correct procedure, but also that they are doing so in a way that is congruent with the culture of the organisation and the vision the head has for the school's future development. So as well as providing an opportunity for coaching and development, the meeting allows an opportunity for alignment.

When a new team member joins then the mode of this coaching meeting will be very different. The new colleague will be learning the ropes – trying to make sense of the school and their new role. The purpose of the meeting will then be about induction, but also with a large degree of direction: there are things that need to be done and they need to be done in a particular way. As time goes on, the mode changes, as shown in Fig. 3.1, which is a familiar representation of situational leadership. Progress through the diagram though is not, as sometimes is indicated, a straightforward journey. So where new activities are demanded then the mode may well return from delegating to directing. This is entirely appropriate.

The coaching model in action

The following four case studies illustrate some of the different ways in which the coaching model presented here can be used. The first case study shows a straightforward progression through the model: starting at directing and moving counter-clockwise through the four boxes. It tells

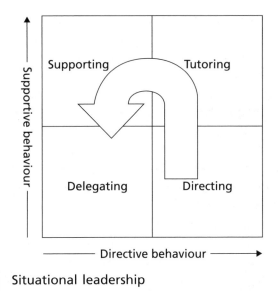

FIG. 3.1 Situational leadership

the story of a newly appointed deputy head learning his trade and so, as it deals with the postholder from initial recruitment through to experienced deputy head, it serves to provide a baseline for how the model can work.

CASE STUDY 1

The new deputy head

Stephen Thompson had always been a very ambitious teacher, working his way up to head of science in a very short time. Highly motivated to lead, he had managed to get himself on to the very first cohort of the National Professional Qualification for Headship (NPQH) while still in his departmental leadership role. Stephen always knew he wanted to lead his own school and planned his career accordingly. Whereas many of his contemporaries decided to get a toehold in a school leadership team by going for the post of assistant head, Stephen was determined that this step would slow his trajectory to the position he really wanted, so decided that the career step he required was deputy head. After some searching Stephen happened across the ideal post. It was a courageous step to take, since it was the deputy headship in a school that had just avoided an Ofsted category and was in a bit of a mess. On the other hand, it was a sole deputy position and the head of the school had only recently moved to the school as her first headship. It was clear to Stephen that here was a school that would provide what he needed to advance his career.

The headteacher of the school, Angela James, recognised Stephen as someone with tremendous raw potential. She had always been very ambitious herself and knew that the school needed someone with ambition and drive to move it on, even if this would sometimes be very uncomfortable for other staff in the school. It was clear that Stephen would respond very well to the development opportunities presented in the school, but it was also clear to Angela that she would need to work closely with Stephen in order harness the energy he presented. In fact, this suited Angela very well: she was very excited about having the opportunity to appoint her own person as deputy head at this early stage and wanted to appoint someone with whom she could work closely as a partner in leading the school. So for Stephen the task was to use the opportunity presented by these circumstances to gain the development he needed to move on to headship in the shortest possible time, while for Angela it was to harness Stephen's ambition and drive to produce school improvement as rapidly as possible.

Here, the power of the performance management and coaching paradigm becomes clear. From the outset there were three dimensions to the coaching that Stephen needed:

1 There were a range of tasks Stephen was required to do of which he had no experience. An example of this was completing the Form 7 return (pupil level annual school census, or PLASC as it has now become). Although in many schools this is now completed by administration staff, at the time it was typically a deputy head's job, and it was one of Stephen's very first tasks (as he started in the school in January). This was a good example of the directing mode of operation. The task involved a number of aspects of work that Stephen had not previously come across. First, he was only barely cognisant of the existence of Form 7 prior to being asked to complete the task. Second, the task involved using the SIMS Form 7 module which, as anyone familiar with that piece of software will know, is not necessarily the most intuitive piece of software ever invented. Third, it involved marshalling the administrative resources of the school in order to complete the task to a very tight deadline.

The task for Angela was straightforward: to give Stephen instructions at a high level of detail so that he could complete the task. Although developmental at the level of ensuring that this input would not be required in future, it was highly directional in the sense that Angela simply had to tell Stephen what to do so that he could then go away and do it. Here Angela was functioning very clearly in the directing box of our coaching paradigm. However, because of the relatively closed nature of this task, Angela was then able to withdraw altogether the following year, leaving the task in the delegating area of the diagram with Stephen requiring no direction and no support.

2 Stephen had come from a position of leading a large department so was well used to the tactics of leadership and management in that setting. However, senior leadership, especially the circumstances of being sole deputy, requires a more subtle skill set. Stephen had been used to operating with a high level of personal interaction with his team. Being head of science meant that he was regarded by his team as the 'person who knows' about science teaching. He had brought about significant improvements in his science department and had done this in part by being an expert practitioner in science pedagogy. But moving into a new role meant that some of the tactics of leadership and management he had been used to using were at best less useful and at worst counter-productive. Stephen's main role was to lead the heads of department – a group of people who had been used to working with almost complete autonomy under the regime prior to Angela and Stephen taking over. Ofsted had placed a large emphasis upon the importance of curriculum planning and leadership and management (which it regarded as unsatisfactory). So, although the heads of department were used to this autonomy, transparently that approach had not worked. Unfortunately, the heads of department team did not recognise that they were part of the problem for the school. Therefore, the second aspect of the task for Angela was to help Stephen develop his approach to leadership and management to ensure that the heads of department team were coaxed and coerced (on some occasions) towards the improvement that was required. Stephen's very direct style from leading his department team provided a very important platform to create the team of heads of department that was required. However, there were occasions where his approach perhaps needed a little more finesse. This is where Angela was able to play an important tutoring role, helping Stephen to acquire the skills required to lead and manage this more disparate team.

Stephen needed to be able to communicate effectively with a team with whom he did not have daily contact – unlike his previous experience as head of department. The fundamental difference Angela could see was that each communication moment with a head of department in the new role was of high significance, so making the style of individual meetings, team meetings and written communications very important. In those first months Angela worked closely with Stephen on preparation for meetings and on reviewing written communications with him. The tutoring approach took the form of a series of probing questions about what Stephen was trying to achieve with his communications. Memos were a good example: Angela would establish what reaction Stephen was hoping to provoke from any particular memo and then encourage him to reflect on whether or not the style of communication was likely to achieve the desired outcome.

Critically important in this aspect of coaching is the response of the coachee. Angela was fortunate that Stephen was hungry for the development and was highly proactive in seeking the tutoring that Angela could provide. It is not uncommon for people to be highly sensitive to criticism of their work, however constructive in intent. If Stephen had been less open-minded and less willing to learn then Angela would have had a much more difficult task in getting him to the point where he was ready to learn from her. With other senior colleagues, Angela found it was sometimes necessary to let them make some fairly big mistakes before they realised that they needed the help she could provide.

This work falls clearly within the tutoring role, requiring large amounts of direction as well as large amounts of support. Angela and Stephen found themselves moving fairly swiftly into the supporting box.

3 The last area of development for Stephen related to alignment of vision. Throughout all the interactions in phase 2 it was clearly the case that Angela was providing guidance on how she wanted the school led and managed, and this would form a very important part of the interactions between Angela and Stephen. But more overtly Angela wanted to harness Stephen's energy in creating the vision and direction of the school. And it was here that they found they could work most creatively together. Through a series of long discussions and debates Angela and Stephen established the destination they desired for the school. Through these debates, the vision for the school became a genuinely shared enterprise, and because of the willingness to challenge each other's thinking the outcome was a very well-thought-through development plan. And it was in this last sense that Angela was really managing Stephen's performance. Through these discussions and debates the exact nature of Stephen's role within that development plan became ever clearer to him, and as a result his work was closely aligned to the key priorities that he had worked out with Angela.

So through the development activities described above we can see a very clear development of both the person, Stephen, and his performance in relation to the school's key priorities. The fundamental importance to his performance of the discussions between Stephen and his line manager – whether these were tutoring, or directing or supporting – cannot be underestimated. Having agreed how Form 7 was going to be completed in phase 1, or how a heads of department meeting would be managed in phase 2, or indeed how the school development plan was going to be expressed, recorded and followed through in phase 3, then the momentum of each of these steps could only be maintained if followed with a subsequent meeting to monitor progress.

Stephen did get his headship and rapidly put in place the same model for performance management with his new team as he had experienced himself.

In this case study we have an example of an interaction that is probably quite rare, i.e. a head working with a new deputy with a very clear congruence of goals: Stephen wished to take advantage of the development on offer in a very active sense and Angela wished to provide that development in order to achieve her objectives for the school.

In the next case study we have a situation that presents more of a challenge for the manager. Here a head of department is being performance-managed by the deputy head. The head of department was very able, but somewhat misguided as a consequence of her immediate previous experience. The significant thing about this case study is the extent to which it provides an object lesson in the success of the coaching paradigm for producing alignment. The head of department, while highly able, had developed a strong view in opposition to some items of school policy. Through skilful handling of the performance management meetings, the deputy head was able to turn this completely around, to the extent that the department leader became an enthusiastic supporter of those policies she had previously rejected.

CASE STUDY 2

The enthusiastic but misguided head of department

Joan Chiswick was a bit of a high flier – she had been promoted to head of English in her school after four years' teaching. She was undoubtedly talented, and this had been spotted by her predecessor, Blake, who sponsored her for the succession when he moved on. Blake and Joan had worked very closely together. Joan had considerable admiration for him and was in some ways a little in awe of him. Together they set out to challenge the orthodoxy in English teaching; for example, creating separate groups for boys and girls to help overcome boys' under-achievement (although this was only for the highest attainers – all the rest of the pupils were in 'mixed ability' mixed gender groups).

Peter was deputy head and Joan's line manager. Peter knew that things were not well in the English department. Attainment was low, but when challenged Blake's response had been 'What do you expect with a majority of boys?' (as the year group had more boys than girls). Blake had moved on to greater things, but Joan was still very much captivated by his approach to leading the depart-ment. Peter could see that Joan was far more talented a leader than Blake had ever been, but he would need to help her break out of some of the very poor practice that was holding the department back.

The relationship here is very much in the tutoring box of the coaching model. Joan knew how to run a department and did not need a directive approach. But she did need to have her assumptions challenged through her meetings with Peter. There was a strong element of tutoring and, in due course, supporting Joan with her work. But perhaps the strongest aspect of the coaching activity that Peter was providing was that of alignment. He was helping Joan to understand the way of working that he needed from her, and helping her to understand how the department needed to work to line up with the expectations of the rest of the school. For example, Peter worked closely with Joan to tackle two major areas of concern:

- The governors wanted to change the approach to grouping of pupils. Hitherto the school had a fairly laissez-faire approach to this – depart-ments pretty much did what they wanted, hence the approach in the English department. Other departments worked in mixed ability groupings, and in others they worked in broad bands. Joan was com-pletely committed to her approach. As with Blake before her, she would talk about providing 'the top set experience' for as many pupils as possible, and the importance of having 'mixed ability' for all the rest so that they did not become discouraged. Now although there are vari-ous views on grouping approaches, the system Blake had come up with and Joan supported seemed a little bizarre from any perspective. So through careful debate and discussion over a period of time Peter was able to encourage Joan to change her view. Naturally, as deputy head, Peter could have simply issued an instruction that this was to be the case, but given Joan's undoubted ability and enthusiasm he was very certain that this was not an approach he wished to take. By discussing the matter he was able to help Joan see the illogicality of her position and so move Joan on to the point where she not only accepted that the grouping strategy should change (as could have happened much more quickly with a straightforward instruction) but became a believer in the new approach and so was able to convince her department that it was the right thing to do.

■ In common with other English departments, Joan's department had a belief that teachers should be unconstrained in what they teach. Despite the national curriculum, the department believed that in essence the job of the English teacher was to teach the books that they liked to teach and try and draw the strands out of that to meet the curriculum requirements if they could. Again this was one of the tenets of Blake's approach. Peter wanted to make sure that there was a consistent approach across the English department. He wanted there to be a proper scheme of work that would ensure pupils had the opportunity to reach the levels they needed to reach. In other words, the curriculum needed to be taught with the interests of the pupils at its heart and not the enthusiasms of each individual teacher. Again, the process of alignment was required. Alongside the normal business of their regular meetings, Peter found time to discuss curriculum theory and principles with Joan. Of course, being a very able young leader Joan lapped this up, and in due course she found her assumptions about effective English teaching being well and truly challenged by Peter, to the extent that, rather like the grouping debate, she became a proselytiser for this new way of looking at structuring her curriculum.

Peter's work with Joan was exceptional. It required him to have a highly defined and justifiable vision of the curriculum and teaching and learning within the school. It then required him to be able to debate and discuss issues based upon this highly defined and refined vision. As a result, he was able to help Joan develop her very high level of raw ability into an equally clear-thinking head of department – ready, in fact, to move on to work with others in the same way.

Of course, in this case study Peter was working with a colleague who was very able, very ambitious and new in post. So although Joan had got it wrong (in relation to the school's objectives) in a couple of areas, fundamentally she was a very good subject leader and so this made Peter's task easier than it might have been. Indeed much easier than the deputy head in the next case study. Here the head of department has been in post for years and has developed an approach with which she is happy – and indeed so is everyone else, judging by the fact that she has been left to get on with it undisturbed for her entire career. What has happened here is that the head of department has moved into the 'delegating' box and has been left there to get on with it. The deputy head has a real challenge: to move this colleague back to 'directing' so that the process that has been under way for the previous 25 years or so can be undone.

CASE STUDY 3

The reluctant head of department

Georgina Tyrell had worked at the Castle School for 27 years – all her career. She had fairly rapidly gained promotion to become head of the geography department and, as she entered her fifties, had a reputation within the school for being an effective practitioner. However, two circumstances arrived to change Georgina's world: first, there was an inspection where her department was judged to be just satisfactory; and, second, at around the time of the inspection there was a new head and deputy appointed by the governors, with a very clear brief to raise standards of attainment in the school.

The inspection in particular was a difficult time for Georgina. Although her own reputation within the school was very strong, the inspection team did not recognise this. Her department was criticised for its lack of curriculum leadership and planning, its inadequate assessment procedures and its pedestrian teaching. How does this square with Georgina's reputation in the school? It is undoubtedly the case that Georgina was a sound colleague – highly reliable, talking the right language to her colleagues about what was wrong with the school and what needed to be improved (mostly the poor behaviour of the children), and as a practitioner herself she experienced no difficulties with classroom management, raising few if any behaviour referrals. In a school that, in general, evaluated classroom practice solely in terms of behaviour, then Georgina appeared to be a very good teacher. It was only with the arrival of Ofsted and the new school management regime that this perspective was challenged.

Georgina's outlook on her work was steeped in the 1970s analysis of teacher professionalism, with the head of department's role principally revolving around resource management (i.e. spending the department capitation) and administration (e.g. entering students for examinations and the like). Attendance at heads of department meetings was important for the profile of the subject and for the heads of department to have an interface with the senior management, but really the meeting was expected to achieve little. In fact Georgina saw her role as a classroom teacher plus, and the plus was not very much – mostly being head of department was something of a reward for having been around for some time.

Unsurprisingly, this was not the way the new leadership of the school saw matters. The new deputy head, Jennifer Bates, arrived not long after the inspection, with the brief to improve the quality of teaching in the school. To facilitate this she was given responsibility for all the heads of department. Georgina presented some particular difficulties. She already thought that she was doing a very good job and so had little reason to change the approach. Added to this was her view that having been head of department for 25 years there was little this new person – who only had experience of teaching English – could show her about teaching and learning in geography. Furthermore, Georgina was convinced that she was already working as hard as she possibly could and so had no capacity to do any more.

Jennifer had a number of tasks in order to be successful with Georgina:

- Georgina needed to be convinced that there was a problem;
- she need to be convinced that given there was a problem that Jennifer could help her with it;
- she needed to be convinced that it was a reasonable expectation of her time to carry out the curriculum development and planning that was to be the solution to the problem.

Of all the meetings with heads of department that Jennifer carried out, Georgina's was always one of the most difficult. In the first months, even getting Georgina to attend was a difficulty, and when she did attend there was a reluctance about engaging in the process, which made each encounter very hard work. Jennifer required considerable tenacity to get through these early encounters. But this is why tenacity is a key attribute for leadership: it is (relatively) easy to lead and manage those who wish to be led and managed, but to take on the reluctant ones is another matter altogether.

Having ensured Georgina attended meetings, what form did the meetings take? The school development plan had been agreed by the heads of department. This is an important part of setting the backdrop to the coaching meeting as it is a common agreed starting point – when the going gets a little difficult the head of department can be reminded that they did agree to the development plan. (However, what happens if the heads of department do not agree to the development plan? It would be our view that this is an unlikely occurrence if the plan is developed and shared with heads of department appropriately.) Georgina had indeed been part of the heads of department group that had agreed to the plan, and so the meeting between Georgina and Jennifer had implementation of the plan as its agenda.

There are no short cuts to progress: it must be taken step by step, managing the objections as they are raised, having the debates about what is required and overcoming the inevitable arguments that this or that suggestion might be 'all very well for other subjects but is impossible in my subject'. It also involves dealing with objections to the increased workload that the suggested development will involve. At the outset, meetings between Georgina and Jennifer were very much focused on direction. Georgina did not see the point of the work Jennifer wanted her to do and did not really understand it either; the consequence of this for Jennifer was that she needed to be very clear and precise about exactly what was to be achieved in time for the next meeting – the task had to be broken down into small digestible chunks. As time went by, Georgina began to see the suggested direction of the work bearing fruit. Other colleagues in the geography department were able to comment upon the schemes of work Georgina had produced and how useful they were. The assessment model that Jennifer suggested was clearly bearing fruit too, since Georgina could see the gains in pupils' learning. As these views developed in Georgina, Jennifer was able to move into the tutoring section of the model, Georgina began to enjoy the meetings (well, almost) and started to think she was developing leading-edge practice in the school. Eventually, Jennifer asked Georgina to present her assessment model in the good practice slot at the heads of department meeting.

This is a great success story, although even at the end of all this Jennifer found that Georgina was never really able to move beyond the tutoring stage. However, when Ofsted came around again, Georgina's department was graded 'Good'. A real result for Georgina – but probably an even bigger one for Jennifer! Jennifer certainly did not look forward to meeting Georgina and producing the improvements in the work was a major effort

– but it did work and in due course Jennifer was able to look back on Georgina as one of her successes. However, this cannot always be taken for granted. Sometimes the member of staff who is being coached and performance-managed either can't or won't produce the necessary improvements. In many ways this last case study might be considered to be just such a situation. Georgina had real difficulty understanding what was expected of her, so she found at first she could not do it – she was also quite reactionary about all these expectations being placed on her and did not really see why she should change. However, in due course she found she could do it and even found she enjoyed working in this new way. By contrast, the colleague in our next case study was simply not able or willing to do what was required. This is an unwelcome position to find ourselves in, but the coaching paradigm is, in many ways, at its most powerful under such circumstances. The repeated meetings create a momentum for change: when a head of department is called back every two to four weeks to account for the progress they have or haven't made, then it becomes increasingly apparent that something has to happen both to the coach and the coachee. This is just what happened in this next case study, which shows how the coaching paradigm can produce a solution to even the most intractable problem.

CASE STUDY 4

The incompetent head of department

Mike White joined the Greenbay School as head of IT. He came well recommended from his previous school. As is common in this particular subject area, he was really a specialist in another subject area – his main subject was technology. As a recruitment incentive (and because the school had something of a budget difficulty), Mike was appointed on a higher scale to lead the technology department as well. This seemed to be fine as he was able to speak knowledgably about both subjects and had the leadership skills required to make them successful.

During Mike's first few months things seemed to be going well. There were a few worries about lateness in the morning and the odd task promised but not completed, but Mike was apparently working very hard and arriving early and leaving late. He was also looking at the development of the school's IT facilities in an innovative way, proposing new technology to cut the unit costs of equipping the school with computers.

The school purchased the new system recommended by Mike – and this is where things started to go wrong. It was not a good buy. The system was untried, and ended up costing much more than Mike's original estimates. There were a range of requirements that Mike had assured the school management team were within the capabilities of the equipment, but there seemed to be no evidence for this. Technical problems plagued the installation, making it unreliable and something of a laughing stock among the pupils.

Mike's line manager was Bill Watson, the deputy head. Bill had been involved in appointing Mike and had worked with him on the new system. Mike had convinced him that this was the system to go with. Bill met regularly with Mike to discuss progress.

In this case study, because of Mike's apparent experience and skill, Bill worked at first in the delegating quadrant, but as time went on it was evident that Mike was having difficulty coping with the work and so Bill moved into the supporting quadrant. Of course, it became apparent as soon as Bill started taking a closer look at what was going on that Mike was really not coping at all well; in fact, it turned out that he had been less than honest on occasions. There were also concerns about his teaching work, with pupils saying that they were not being taught anything, Mike claimed that he had done things with his classes when he hadn't, he missed deadlines and was not carrying out basic work like writing reports and so forth. Here was someone who seemed to be going under. Bill needed to take a much closer interest in what was going on, and so moved into tutoring mode. Meetings became more frequent, but this meant that Mike began to feel as though he was not being trusted – which of course he wasn't. Mike's professional pride started getting in the way, to the extent that Bill moved right back into the directing quadrant. In contrast to their early work together, where Mike would be informing Bill what was happening, now Bill was setting the agenda very clearly. Meetings were recorded with actions agreed and deadlines. Sadly, for one reason or another, Mike could not seem to organise himself to meet any of the requirements of his post. In due course the whole coaching process was suspended and a competence procedure ensued. Mike resigned 18 months after he took up his post.

The benefits of the coaching paradigm

The coaching paradigm presented at the beginning of this chapter has been illustrated in action through these four case studies. They have demonstrated the paradigm not only as a method for achieving the goal of consistent performance management on an ongoing basis, but also as an approach for managing the whole school, or indeed any other organisation. By providing a frequent, timetabled, regular contact between the manager and the managed then we have an approach that creates a momentum for school improvement that is unstoppable. Frequently colleagues who experience these meetings for the first time can react against them. The prospect of meeting with their line manager each week, fortnight or whatever makes them think they are not trusted and that they are being checked up on. But it is our experience that these same people soon come to value the interaction, because even in difficult situations (as in the last case study) it is ultimately a method of securing accountability and the required standard of performance, while in more normal circumstances it demonstrates to colleagues that their work is important. Accountability is not only something that managers want from their team, it is something their team wants too. Effective practitioners want to be held to account for their work because it shows their managers that they are doing a good job, and then they get the recognition they deserve for what they do. In fact, once all the players are used to the regular meetings then they become something that team members require and indeed miss if they don't happen.

Conclusion

In conclusion, there are some factors that are crucial in order to make the coaching process effective. Most importantly, the team leader must take the meetings seriously. They must prioritise them over other matters, so if a regular meeting has to be cancelled due to other commitments then the meeting must be rescheduled for the same week. Never let a meeting lapse, because only too quickly many will have lapsed and the team will begin to treat the whole business with scepticism. Furthermore, the allotted time must not be curtailed – unless it genuinely is the case that the meeting has run its course. Even under these circumstances it is often the case that some of the most useful discussion can transpire by raising the horizon of the discussion above the immediate concerns to the more strategic nature of the team members' role. Stephen Covey (1989) talks of synergy as being one of the seven habits of highly effective people. It is often when the main agenda of a meeting has run its course that there is a good opportunity for synergy.

At the meeting it is reasonable for the team leader to expect the team member to bring an agenda of things they wish to discuss. Where possible, their agenda should be dealt with first – this avoids the impression of the meeting being a time when people show up to receive their orders. If this is the way meetings are structured then it makes it even more powerful when a team leader starts the meeting with whatever is on their mind. During the discussion it is wise to avoid giving answers. Where members of the team have difficulty with something they are trying to achieve, then as far as is possible they should be helped to think the problem through themselves. This is the developmental aspect of the activity, moving them through the boxes of the diagram.

Finally, there are different views on recording the meetings. Certainly under the circumstances of the last case study then everything needs to be recorded in detail, but even under more benign circumstances it is useful to have a record of the process. Of course, this can create a very large amount of work for each team leader, so one solution – which also has the benefit of being developmental – is to ask the team member to provide the minutes of each meeting. Critically, action points agreed at each meeting must be recorded.

We strongly believe this approach to coaching, development and management is a highly effective method of monitoring, creating accountability and, most importantly, exercising the leadership of the team leader. Through this system it is possible to create a high-performing team aligned and united by a shared vision and common purpose.

Reference

Covey, S. (1989) *The Seven Habits of Highly Effective People*, Simon & Schuster, London.

chapter four

Creating job descriptions

The legal position

Creating an effective job description

Title of the job

Grading and pay

Core purpose

From core purpose to specifics

Support staff

Conclusion

Why do job descriptions matter to people? Frequently people will say 'I've never had a job description', or 'I think my job description needs to be reviewed', or even 'It's not included in my job description'. It is almost as if having a job description is some kind of panacea that addresses any inequalities, inequities or inadequacies and that once it is in place then all will be well. Of course there is an obligation on the part of school leaders to provide people with an up-to-date job description – how else can people know what is expected of them? And the central theme of this book is that people should know what is expected of them through the performance management process, and that through the support of regular dialogue about an individual's performance we achieve organisational goals. Certainly, the responsibilities, tasks, outcomes and accountabilities need to be set down somewhere, but they should be regarded as a safety net for both sides of the performance management relationship.

Job descriptions vary from the vague to the pedantic and it is useful to consider who benefits from either ends of this particular spectrum. If the job description is very vague then both sides can choose to preserve this vagueness, or when the going gets tough use it to prescribe. Of course, this may end up being subjected to legal scrutiny and either side may end up losing. A vague document leads to confusion and the outcome is always messy. Alternatively, the highly prescriptive and didactic document can have the opposite effect. If everything that is expected is presumed to be recorded in the job description then the document will either be a tome or will have missed something out. There is a danger that an individual will claim that since everything else was specified in detail, any omission was deliberate. Or, if the document is a tome, then the production of the job description becomes an end in itself and certainly the outcome can never be seen as a working document.

The legal position

From a legal point of view, the guidance is somewhat sketchy. According to Croner's *Teachers' Rights, Duties and Responsibilities*, a newly appointed teacher should receive a job description around the same time as their letter of appointment. It may be fairly short, giving a job title, statutory duties and a general job description, or it may be a detailed list of tasks.

The law of education is often less than precise, although it is given some clarity through various tests and case law – though examples relating to job descriptions are sparse. The High Court in *Sim* v. *Rotherham MBC* (1986) held that teachers were members of a profession where obligations were not confined to imparting academic knowledge. Each teacher has a duty to cooperate in the running of the school, according to direction given by the headteacher. Since then, of course, the major categories of a teacher's conditions of employment have been laid down in the annual School Teachers' Pay and Conditions Document (STPCD).

The STPCD is quite a lengthy document and, as befits a piece of statute, has its fair share of 'subject to paragraph . . .' and 'in accordance with . . .'. However, it does form the basis for teachers' job descriptions and sets down some important responsibilities and accountabilities. The majority of the statements refer to conditions of service affecting every- one who is employed as a teacher at a school (the exceptions being the headteacher and the deputy headteachers). In our view, the job descrip- tion should be personalised for the individual teacher to give guidance on the responsibilities and accountabilities of the individual role. This is because the main emphasis of this book is that schools should develop their own policies and practices. However, generic expectations can still be relevant to this deliberation.

The Conditions of Employment form Part XII in the STPCD. There are a number of sections:

- *Exercise of general professional duties*. Teachers should exercise general pro- fessional duties under the reasonable direction of the headteacher. This is an important opening statement because it means that if the duty is reasonable the headteacher can direct the teacher to do it and con- sequently if the person refuses they are in breach of the one of the con- ditions of service. Of course, whether the duty is reasonable is a particular question that is challenged in both informal and formal hearings.

- *Exercise of particular duties*. Again, the opening statement indicates that the headteacher may change a person's duties from time to time. This is an important point because if the job description is set down at the time of appointment, then circumstances change and there needs to be sufficient flexibility to allocate other duties to a teacher. Again, this has to be reasonable.

- *Professional duties*. Teachers are required to plan and prepare courses and lessons, teach pupils that have been assigned to the teacher, and set and mark work carried out by the pupil in school and elsewhere. Teachers are required, therefore, to plan and teach children and mark their work – whether this is classwork or homework or wherever it is done. In addition, teachers must assess, record and report on pupils' progress and attainment.

- *Other activities*. Teachers are required to provide advice to pupils about their careers, keep records, communicate and consult with parents and other bodies, and participate in meetings arranged for these purposes.

- *Appraisal*. Teachers are required to participate in the arrangements for their own appraisal and that of others.

- *Review induction, further training and development*. Teachers are required to review their methods of teaching and programmes of work and participate in arrangements for further training and professional development as a teacher, including undertaking training and professional development that aim to meet needs identified in appraisal objectives or in appraisal statements.

- *Educational methods*. Teachers are required to advise and cooperate with other teachers on the preparation and development of courses of study, teaching materials, teaching programmes, methods of teaching, assessment and pastoral arrangements.

- *Discipline, health and safety*. Teachers are required to maintain good order and discipline among pupils.

- *Staff meetings*. Teachers are required to participate in meetings at the school that relate to the curriculum of the school or the administration or organisation of the school, including pastoral arrangements.

- *Cover*. Teachers are required to supervise and so far as practicable teach any pupils whose teacher is not available to teach them (this is subject to an upper limit of 38 hours in any school year).

- *Public examinations*. Teachers are required to participate in arrangements for preparing pupils for public examinations, assess pupils for the purposes of such examinations, record and report such assessments, and participate in arrangements for pupils' presentation for and supervision during such examinations.

- *Management*. Teachers are required to contribute to the selection for appointment and professional development of other teachers and support staff, including the induction and assessment of new teachers and teachers serving induction periods pursuant to the induction regulations; teachers can also be required to coordinate or manage the work of other staff.

So, summing all of this information, all teachers are required to work together (contribute to meetings, work together on schemes of work, cover for colleagues, etc.), teach and assess the work of pupils, advise parents of progress, keep order and undertake development activities so that they can improve. However, it is when these general conditions of service need to be specified more precisely that the job description comes to the fore.

Creating an effective job description

The job description can give guidance on how the teacher, or more generally the employee, should fulfil their responsibilities. It can vary from a detailed list of tasks to a general job description. We believe that neither of these extremes is useful; employees need sufficient guidance to structure their operational responsibilities, sufficient flexibility in this guidance to enable them to take decisions without necessary referral, but absolute clarity on what outcomes are required and the level of accountability that the role demands.

There are a number of elements that are essential to an effective and useful job description:

- title of the job
- grade
- accountability relationship
- core purpose
- tasks, responsibilities and outcomes.

Title of the job

The title of the job might seem to be the most unproblematic section of the job description, but some people do get very exercised about it. Schools organised on traditional lines of communication will typically use titles such as 'head of . . .'. The person who is head of English, for example, will have responsibility for anything with the word English attached to it. The title has overtones of a hierarchical model in which:

- communications are via the head of department;
- problems are raised with the head of department;
- authority for the subject rests with the head of department.

Some schools group subjects together and create roles such as the head of faculty. This is often used when a number of subjects are brought together under a single person's responsibility. Examples of this are expressive arts (usually music, drama and art), humanities (history, geography and sociology) and science (biology, chemistry and physics). Often these individual subjects may have heads of departments as well. By grouping subjects together, the head of faculty role may represent:

- a collegial model where opportunities exist for collaboration;
- a recognition that those who work in small departments (where there is one or two staff only) need opportunities to work with others.

Many secondary schools will have heads of year. These people are typically responsible for the pastoral welfare of a cohort of pupils. This may be according to the ages of the students (i.e. head of year 7 etc.) or may be vertical groups (this occurs where there is a house system in the school). The existence of this title may suggest a pastoral/academic divide. In this case the heads of subject deal with the academic issues and year heads deal with behaviour. There are often committees and groups where these two groups are brought together to address an issue. Too often, this split is a problem for many schools, for example because:

- year heads may be paid at a lower point on the scale than heads of department;
- year heads often will have considerable power, simply because they will have the responsibility for behaviour of the students;
- department heads will be powerful in a different way – controlling large parts of the school's budget and the direction of teachers.

Some schools will use the descriptor 'coordinator', for example a subject coordinator. This term is used widely in primary schools where a named teacher is responsible for the subject in the school, but all teachers in the school teach the subject. In small schools, all the teachers will have such a title, and may have several – i.e. subject coordinator for maths and PE. This type of job reflects the way in which primary school teachers function. The primary school teacher will have responsibility for the class they teach; they will teach that class for all subjects (with some exceptions, depending on expertise and the size of the school, etc.). Primary school teachers are typically child-centred and see the class as 'my class'. Thus the term 'coordinator' reflects the autonomy that the teacher has in their classroom.

Roles that do not fit neatly into traditional hierarchical structures (where the 'head of . . .' role sums things up nicely) will often use the title 'director of . . .'. This title is used in several contexts – usually where there is a particular characteristic of the role that separates it from others. For example, the title is used to identify director of sixth form, director of music, cross-curricular director, director of studies, etc. In schools where these terms are used they have been introduced for the following reasons:

- to enhance the status of the head of music (for example);
- to acknowledge the different role that a director may have – for example, their responsibilities include extra-curricular activities (i.e. sports fixtures, choirs, orchestras, etc.);
- to differentiate the head of sixth from other pastoral heads;
- to signify a role difference for the director of sixth form – this person will often have academic and pastoral responsibility;
- to reflect the status of such roles as 'cross-curricular director' or 'director of studies' (in terms of responsibility points);
- to acknowledge that a head of subject is also responsible for the school's specialism (or, for example, if the school is a specialist technology college then the head of technology's enhanced role might be recognised in the title).

Titles and what we call people

Titles do matter – not only because they give clues to the way in which the organisation is structured but also because they convey much about the power relationships in the organisation. However, there is an important consideration to be made when deciding what to call people (note that we use this phrase deliberately, because the job is the person). This is that a hierarchical structure is not incompatible with distributed leadership. At the same time, a flat structure (where a number of people have the same graded job and are equally represented in policy-making bodies) is not a quick-fix way to make the organisation run on distributed leadership principles. Distributed leadership is far more subtle than that.

Schools are incredibly political places. In his famous work on the micro-politics of the school, Ball (1987) talks about the relationships between heads of departments and describes how those who lead the core departments (i.e. English, mathematics and science) have more power in the organisation than smaller departments. While organisations may undertake a whole range of strategies and programmes to obviate these issues, school life remains essentially political. Working together productively in schools depends on positive relationships. When teachers come together as a whole staff, or in departments, or indeed in teams (such as the head of year or heads of department teams), a dynamic of relationships is created. The relationships are subject to many forces. Stoll et al. (2001) list the following forces as determinants in the school learning context:

- particular mix of pupils;
- relationships;
- morale;
- history;
- culture;
- micro-politics;
- support staff;
- structures;
- leadership.

So as we examine the need for job descriptions it is essential that we are aware of the various forces that affect the social construct of our schools.

Deciding what to call a job and what someone will do

What we call postholders is a sign of the deeper levels of assumptions shared by members – how people respond to the names we give to roles brings the unconscious operational culture to the surface and requires the organisation to discuss and debate how the school sees itself. The following case study introduces some of the principles of job construction in the context of school improvement, and we use Stoll's model (2001) to consider the issues.

CASE STUDY

Bradbury High School has just over 1000 pupils but its post-16 stay-on rate is poor. Currently there are 52 students in Years 12 and 13. Peter, the headteacher, is keen to improve the post-16 curriculum and increase the number of students who stay at the school after the age of 16 – and the governing body is very anxious that this should happen. As he considers the proposal he wants to put to the governors, Peter thinks that a post of responsibility needs to be created to address this issue as there is insufficient capacity in other areas of the school to accommodate the brief. Should this be a leadership team appointment or an opportunity for a promoted post with an appropriate allowance? What title should be given to this post – so that it conveys the strategic importance of the role?

The thinking that will determine the recommendation to the governors is critical to how successful the role will be. Put simply, if the role is not sufficiently clearly expressed then there will be confusion in the school and the opportunity for development will be at best slow and at worst stifled by debate on what should actually be happening. If we use Stoll's model to consider the issues then the questions such a change creates will emerge.

- *Particular mix of pupils*. The kind of role that is created to bring about a change in the post-16 provision in the school will depend to a very large extent on the particular mix of the pupils. How do people see the pupils (do they see them as problems to be addressed or the most important people in the school)? How people at Bradbury School regard the current sixth form will say much about the potential to bring about change. In one school known to us, A-level teaching was considered a prize for the most senior members of staff – teachers who were given a year 12 or 13 tutor group were congratulated because it was regarded as a promotion (but not remunerated!). To bring about a seismic change in approach to the sixth form will require a strategic plan that has the endorsement of the leadership team in general and the headteacher in particular. The question to be asked is why do we want an enlarged sixth form: is it because we want more children to have the post-16 opportunity, or is it that we do not offer sufficient opportunities for our students post-16 and want to address their needs?

- *Relationships*. What impact will a new post have on the existing relationships? At one school the proposal to create a head of sixth form was met with much dismay – not because there was any sense that this was not an appropriate role but because some people felt that 'they didn't want more people above them'. Some might reject this as nonsense, but a perception that change is about creating a hierarchy says much about people's perceptions of the structure in the school. In this example it was resolved by calling the post 'sixth form coordinator', but as the headteacher told us several months into the appointment: 'We wish we'd stuck it out and called the post "head of sixth form" – the post hasn't really gone in the direction we want because it has been too much about coordination and less about leadership'. Titles do matter and it can be useful when changing the structure to make a particular point through the title that is given to a role. The title does not change the role, but it might change people's perception of what the role is out to achieve.

- *Morale.* The morale of the organisation can be affected by the way in which the change is brought about. By making a case for a strategic change in the way in which the post-16 sector of the school functions, the head of Bradbury School is setting down a marker that has the potential to bring about a major change in the school's perception of itself. How the role is presented to the community, outside the staffroom, will have a significant impact on how people see the change.

- *History.* The historical nature of post-16 provisions at Bradbury School needs to be considered. That there is currently no one responsible for the sixth form makes a sharp statement about priorities at the school. Assigning a member of the leadership team responsibility for an area of the school immediately raises its profile. How the sixth form has been managed over time is part of the consideration – if a real difference is to be brought about, then making a very clear change in the way in which the sixth form is led is essential. However, a school that simply wants to build on its existing provision can afford to take a 'softer' approach and pursue the 'convenor' or 'coordinator' title.

- *Culture and structures.* Culturally, changing the structure of the staffing in this way leads to a shift in organisational emphasis. If the reaction of some staff is to express concern at another layer of management then a debate on structures needs to be had. According to Fullan (1993), attempts to bring about improvement that do not address school culture can be see as 'doomed to tinkering' – we cannot bring about change at any significant level unless we are prepared to address the way in which the school operates. Of course, one way to change the way the school operates is to bring about changes in the structures, but these need to be reinforced through a range of other levers (for example, if a school wants to bring about a closer relationship between heads of year and heads of department, one way to do this is to hold joint meetings).

- *Micro-politics.* Schools are political places and so decisions on job titles will be seen in a political context – if all the academic posts have 'head of . . .' titles and the pastoral posts are 'year 7 coordinator' then any new post that is either a 'head of . . .' or '. . . coordinator' will be associated with one dimension or the other.

What we call things does matter because, when we look at the pieces of paper that are the artefacts of our schools, they convey so much about what we want to say about the organisation and how it interrelates.

—————— Grading and pay ——————

We cannot talk about job descriptions and titles for long without considering the issues of grading and pay. This conversation is, of course, about power relationships but also about the remuneration people receive for the jobs they undertake.

The recent change from management allowances to teaching and learning responsibility (TLR) payments have brought the issue of grading to the fore. The scheme of management allowances comprised five allowances that were awarded for a range of responsibilities and duties. The cash value of the allowances was frozen in the STPCD 2004 settlement. The purpose of this freeze was to enable schools to undertake the necessary restructuring that would bring together the National Agreement *Raising Standards and Tackling Workload*, which is leading to a removal of administrative tasks from a teacher's job. All teachers in receipt of allowances for administrative roles are to be offered new responsibilities, with no detriment to their pay and conditions.

As well as the National Agreement there is a requirement on all schools to restructure in order to direct remunerated responsibilities to teaching and learning. Schools have to have a pay policy in place and restructure their teaching staff. Staff who face a drop in salary will have their allowance protected for three years. The entire process must be completed in three years. One purpose of the legislation is to give schools the opportunity to restructure and to have more flexible pay structures that enable them to remunerate teachers for teaching and learning activities, or, in other words, to ensure that schools only remunerate teachers for activity focused on teaching and learning. Schools need to establish a process for this restructuring and deciding what will be done. There are two bands for TLR: TLR1 and TLR2. There has to be a clear distinction between the responsibility for TLR1 payments and TLR2 remuneration. The principal distinction is for significant responsibility for other staff – if a post does not have this level of responsibility it cannot be remunerated at TLR1 level.

One way to proceed is to draw up roles using the descriptors in the legislation. These are:

- leading, managing and developing a subject or curriculum area or pupil development across the curriculum;
- impact on educational progress of pupils beyond those assigned to the teacher;
- leading, developing and enhancing the teaching practice of others and managing staff;
- monitoring and accountability.

By associating activities with these headings it is possible to see the relative strengths of different roles.

Schools can either decide how they want to remunerate posts and write roles that satisfy the criteria, or compile roles and then see what level of remuneration is appropriate. Of course, the latter risks creating a structure that the school cannot afford, but the former could mean that the school misses out on the opportunity to rethink its structures. In reality, the process is less straightforward than either of these two choices – we have to create the structure we want that will achieve the organisational goals, but the bill does have to be paid.

Core purpose

The first step in creating the structure is to look at the core purpose of the job. Ask the question: why do we want this job to be done in the school? Sometimes another question can help: if the person doing the job left, would we replace the postholder? This may focus the mind on what the core purpose of the role is. Another question is: what is the principal outcome of the role? In the case of the headteacher, the National Standards for headteachers (issued by the DfES) offer a useful model:

The headteacher is the leading professional in the school. Accountable to the governing body, the headteacher provides vision, leadership and direction for the school and ensures that it is managed and organised to meet its aims and targets. The headteacher, working with others, is responsible for:

- *evaluating the school's performance to identify the priorities for continuous improvement and raising standards; ensuring equality of opportunity for all;*
- *developing policies and practices; ensuring that resources are efficiently and effectively used to achieve the school's aims and objectives and for the day-to-day management, organisation and administration of the school.*

The headteacher, working with and through others, secures the commitment of the wider community to the school by developing and maintaining effective partnerships with, for example, schools, other services and agencies for children, the LEA, higher education institutions and employers. Through such partnerships and other activities, headteachers play a key role in contributing to the development of the education system as a whole and collaborate with others to raise standards locally.

Drawing on the support provided by members of the school community, the headteacher is responsible for creating a productive learning environment which is engaging and fulfilling for all pupils.

This description of the headteacher's core purpose is quite long and our advice for most roles would be to try to summarise the role in one or two sentences. So for a class teacher this might be something like: 'The core purpose of a classroom teacher is to contribute, as an individual and part of a team, to the realisation of the aims of the school.' Of course, one immediate drawback with this core purpose is that broadly it is applicable to anyone who works in the school – it applies equally to class teachers, catering staff, secretaries, teaching assistants and other staff. Some further illustration of the role of the teacher is probably necessary.

In many ways the core purpose gets a little easier with promoted posts because then we can talk about the additional role that the individual carries out beyond the common role of class teacher. So for a head of year the core purpose might read:

- *To provide professional leadership and management for a group of pupils to secure high levels of behaviour, promote high levels of ambition and the promotion of independent learning.*

- *To provide leadership and direction for the year group and ensure that it is managed and organised in such a way to meet the aims and objectives of the school.*

- *To play a key role in supporting, guiding and motivating pupils, evaluating the effectiveness of the curriculum provision and the outcomes of learning for their year group and progress towards targets, and informing future priorities for their year group.*

- *To identify needs in their own year group, recognising that these must be considered in relation to the overall needs of the school.*

By articulating the core purpose in this way, a clear performance relationship is set down – the year leader's role is clearly associated with behaviour, ambition and independent learning of pupils. There is also a requirement to lead and manage, and to evaluate the effectiveness of curriculum provision.

This kind of model can be applied to other roles in the school. For sample job descriptions, see the Appendix on page 171.

_____ From core purpose to specifics _____

To create meaningful job descriptions that avoid the too vague or too prescriptive, it is important to include the specific tasks and responsibilities of the post, and also to specify the outcomes that are associated with the role. To illustrate this, consider the job description for a year leader. A specific element of the job description is to have an impact on the educational progress of pupils beyond those assigned to the teacher (this is an essential descriptor for the award of a TLR payment). For the year leader to have this impact, there are tasks and activities that need to be undertaken, but even more critical are the outcomes. In each case the outcomes can be measured in some way. The job description states:

The outcomes that are associated with this element are to lead a year group so that pupils will:

- _actively participate in extra-curricular activities;_
- _achieve high standards in public examinations;_
- _progress to the next stage of their education with confidence and enthusiasm;_
- _show sustained improvement across their subjects;_
- _make informed choices about their future studies;_
- _understand how to improve their studies;_
- _know their academic targets;_
- _show improvement in their literacy, numeracy and information technology skills;_
- _be well prepared for any tests and examinations;_
- _be enthusiastic about school;_
- _contribute to the maintenance of a purposeful working environment._

The easy outcome here is the standards in public examinations, but these include activities along the way – guiding choice for key stage 4 options for example, which is a task often undertaken by heads of year in comprehensive schools. The task remains the same – to manage the options process – but outcomes are now specified: that the students make informed choices (which can be measured through interview, survey, completion rates and so on). Of course, if one outcome is that children know their academic targets, then the head of year will need to know what those targets are and be instrumental in managing the process of sharing these with students. It moves the head of year role away from one that is focused solely on activity (and heads of year postholders often have very reactive jobs as they deal with incidents involving naughty children and poor attenders!).

To make this move from a process that is just about the management of tasks and activities, the next section has been included in the job description:

The outcomes that are associated with this element are to ensure that the teachers and support staff who work with the cohort:

- *are well informed about the cohort's targets;*
- *are well informed about the cohort's progress at the individual and cohort level;*
- *are challenged and supported where individuals and groups are making insufficient progress.*

This section of the job description sets down a belief that one of the ways that the teacher will have an impact on the cohort is through the work of the other members of staff who engage with the pupils. Therefore, there is a requirement for the postholder to communicate information with other people, so that others are well informed and provide the appropriate level of challenge to pupils. Of course, an important relationship is that with parents, which is covered in the next section:

The outcomes that are associated with this element are to ensure that the parents and carers of the cohort:

- *are well informed about their child's achievements at school;*
- *are well informed about their child's targets for improvement;*
- *know the expectations made of their child in relation to their studies, their attendance, behaviour and conduct at school;*
- *know how they can support or assist their child's progress at school.*

Going through this process allows us to rethink what we want postholders to do. By thinking about the core purpose we gain some clarity about why we have these roles, while making the distinction between task and outcome means we can develop a job description with performance objectives. We can now specify:

- pupil performance, relating to the subject or curriculum area, or pupil development across the curriculum;

- the quality of monitoring, evaluation and review required for a role focusing on teaching and learning.

The criteria for the performance review of the TLR aspect of the teacher's role will be grouped under such headings as:

- impact on educational progress of pupils beyond those assigned to the teacher;
- monitoring and accountability;
- significant, sustained and specified high performance over the review period.

Creating a TLR model

Of course, in setting down the job description the vexed question of the TLR tariff still remains. There are many ways in which the TLR cake can be sliced and what is really important is that it is the result of discussion and agreement. There is so much potential for disagreement (pay is always a contentious issue!) that we present just one possible model that can be adapted to other circumstances.

The model is constructed under the following headings:

- leading, managing and developing a subject or curriculum area or pupil development across the curriculum;
- impact on educational progress of pupils beyond those assigned to the teacher;
- leading, developing and enhancing the teaching practice of others and managing staff;
- line responsibility for staff;
- monitoring and accountability.

The rationale for this model is that by having job descriptions compiled under these headings there is then a correspondence between the job description and the tariff. In Table 4.1 the allowances have been included for illustrative purposes, according to the recommended differential between payments for TLR.

Advantages and disadvantages of the model

There are some disadvantages to this model. The first is that by setting out a differential based on the number of pupils who study a subject then

TABLE 4.1 Setting the TLR tariff

Grade	Allowance	Leading, managing and developing a subject or curriculum area or pupil development across the curriculum	Impact on educational progress of pupils beyond those assigned to the teacher	Leading, developing and enhancing the teaching practice of others and managing staff	Line responsibility for staff	Monitoring and accountability
TLR2	£x	■ Leading a cross-curricular project ■ Budgeting for the project	■ Pupil population drawn from across the school	■ Responsibility for staff management over the period of a project	■ Health and safety for relevant areas	■ Annual report and evaluation
TLR2	£x+1500	■ Leading a subject that is followed and assessed by students at key stage 3 (KS3) and KS4. ■ Planning, budgeting and implementing strategies for raising standards in the subject or cohort	■ Attainment targets for each key stage ■ Recruitment targets for KS4 and/or KS5	■ Performance management responsibility for nominated staff	■ Personnel responsibility for nominated staff ■ Up to four full-time or full-time equivalent (fte) teaching staff ■ Up to two full-time (or fte) support staff ■ Health and safety for subject areas	■ Performance review of nominated staff ■ Annual health and safety review ■ Annual public examinations analysis ■ Annual department self-evaluation
TLR2	£x+3000	■ Leading a National Curriculum subject that is compulsory for all students at KS3 and is selected at KS4 by at least 50% of the cohort and 15% of KS5 students ■ Planning, budgeting and implementing strategies for raising standards in the subject	■ Attainment and performance targets for each key stage ■ Recruitment targets for KS4 and/or KS5 ■ Performance management responsibility for nominated staff	■ Extra curricular activities to improve pupil attainment ■ Whole school responsibility for teaching and learning – this might be a project	■ Personnel responsibility for nominated staff ■ Up to two full-time (or fte) support staff ■ Performance review of nominated staff ■ Health and safety for subject areas	■ Performance review of nominated staff ■ Annual health and safety review ■ Annual public examinations analysis ■ Annual department self-evaluation

TABLE 4.1 (cont'd)

Grade	Allowance	Leading, managing and developing a subject or curriculum area or pupil development across the curriculum	Impact on educational progress of pupils beyond those assigned to the teacher	Leading, developing and enhancing the teaching practice of others and managing staff	Line responsibility for staff	Monitoring and accountability
TLR2	£x+3000	■ Leading a year group ■ Planning, budgeting and implementing strategies for raising standards in the cohort	■ Attainment and performance targets for each key stage	■ Year group activities to improve pupil attainment ■ Whole school responsibility for managing pupil behaviour and welfare ■ Tutor team	■ Health and safety for year areas	■ Annual cohort progress report
TLR1	£y	■ Leading a National Curriculum subject that is compulsory for all students or is selected at KS4 by at least 80% of the cohort and 15% of KS5 students ■ Planning, budgeting and implementing strategies for raising standards in the subject or cohort	■ Attainment targets for each key stage ■ Recruitment targets for KS4 and KS5	■ Leading, developing and enhancing the practice of subject staff ■ Whole school responsibility for teaching and learning, staff development, ITT	■ More than four full-time (or fte) teaching ■ Personnel responsibility for nominated staff ■ Performance management responsibility for nominated staff ■ Health and safety for subject areas	■ Performance review of nominated staff ■ Annual health and safety review ■ Annual public examinations analysis ■ Annual department self-evaluation

for optional subjects this increases the competitive nature of the options process and might lead to an overall inflation in one subject to the detriment of another. We know of schools where history and geography, for example, have tended to oscillate their recruitment – one year there might be three history groups and two geography, the following year the position is reversed. The flexibility to remunerate based on subject strength could lead to unacceptable variation in pay. There is perhaps a need to take a longer-term view where remuneration levels are reviewed over a period so that the local fluctuations do not bring about unhealthy competition.

However, the model also has advantages. In particular, it creates a system where responsibility is focused clearly on teaching and learning activity. Although the technical aspects of the restructuring are considerable (and of course will be subject to change), the principles that govern the change have the capacity to bring about advantage and flexibility for all.

Support staff

One of the drivers for change to the way in which teachers are remunerated has been the *Raising Standards and Tackling Workload* National Agreement, which stipulated that teachers cannot be directed to undertake certain administrative tasks. This has brought about, in most schools, an increase in the number of administrative and support staff. Instead of paying a teacher a management allowance for dealing with the buses or the exams, schools now have to make other arrangements to manage these essential tasks that are not focused on teaching and learning. Having discussed in some detail the issues of creating a job description for a teacher with a post of responsibility, our attention must therefore now turn to the support staff.

The support staff in schools include a wide range of people with very different jobs, including catering staff, cleaners, personal assistants, reprographics staff, the bursar, teaching assistants, counsellors and indeed the business manager. These people fulfil very different roles in the school and yet are grouped together to form the support staff. In fact the very term is problematic, but there seems to be no generic title that encompasses the full range of responsibilities that these people undertake: administration staff does not fit the range of tasks, while 'non-teachers' or AOTs (adults other than teachers) seem to be vaguely insulting by describing what someone doesn't do rather than what they do. Perhaps the problem is trying to group people together and so it may be better to think about smaller teams – the finance team, office team, student services team and so on.

Thinking about individual teams in this way also facilitates a discussion about outcomes. For many who work in support roles it may be difficult to see how their own contribution supports the core function of the school, which is to educate students. However, by discussing the core values that are associated with the team structure then outcomes for a group can be agreed. For example, the following illustration shows the outcomes agreed for a group of secretarial and personal assistant staff:

The outcomes that are associated with this role are to work as part of the team of PAs who:

- *are consistent in their practice;*
- *share good practice with other members of staff;*
- *act as role models in managing clients effectively;*
- *act as role models in demonstrating professional administrative support.*

There is a similarity here with the work of the team in the job description of year leader (in the Appendix, see page 180), for example where team outcomes are expressed thus:

Work as a team of year leaders who:

- *are consistent in their practice;*
- *act as role models in managing pupils effectively;*
- *provide training, development and coaching for staff.*

As well as team outcomes, there are specific outcomes associated with a particular role. In the case of a head of subject these are, for example:

The outcomes that are associated with this element are to lead a subject so that pupils will:

- *actively participate in learning;*
- *produce work and assignments in response to curriculum demands (including homework);*
- *conform to the school's behaviour policy.*

As we discussed at the beginning of this chapter, the function of the job description is to be sufficiently descriptive to give direction but not be so prescriptive that it inhibits either the line manager or the postholder. In the case of support staff who frequently will have very distinct roles with no crossover of tasks (for example, a school bursar will often work alone and have a huge bank of knowledge about procedures that no one else will share) it is necessary to create outcomes related to the specific role. For example:

The outcomes associated with the specific role are that there is:

- *effective communication;*
- *a proactive approach to meeting the needs of stakeholders;*
- *an individual and team belief in continuous improvement, which is evidenced through activity;*
- *planned and coordinated work schedules;*
- *effective management of problems;*
- *effective teamwork, where everyone is treated with dignity and respect.*

Conclusion

The methodology we offer for producing job descriptions is one that starts with the core purpose, moves to a description of the tasks and activities, and culminates in outcome statements. The model from Stoll et al. (2001) provides a framework for the range of issues that emerge when we have these discussions. What we choose to call postholders says much about our schools and how we choose to describe the relationships between groups of people is the starting point to how the relationships will eventually be constructed and operate. These decisions affect the social structures that make up what are human organisations.

The debate over teaching and learning responsibility (TLR) payments remains important because these are the way forward for teachers to focus on teaching and learning tasks and for new responsibilities to be located on support staff. Job descriptions are not an end in themselves, but if there is a strong link between the outcomes and performance criteria then a school can create a coherent structure that is a lever to bring about change.

The model we advocate brings into the discussion a number of different issues:

- *The pupils.* What impact will the new job have on the education of the pupils?

- *Relationships.* What impact will a new post have on the existing relationships?

- *How the change is managed.* What impact will a role have on the community's perception of itself?

- *Historical considerations.* Does a role represent clear water between the present and the future, or is it a progression from what is currently offered?

- *Organisational emphasis.* Does the role represent a cultural change in the way the school is working or sees its future direction?

Deciding on the level of remuneration is another matter entirely and must be considered not only within the context of the staffing structure but also in relation to local and national pressures. For clarity, we suggest that job descriptions are drawn up using the following headings:

- leading, managing and developing a subject or curriculum area or pupil development across the curriculum;

- impact on educational progress of pupils beyond those assigned to the teacher;

- leading, developing and enhancing the teaching practice of others and managing staff;

- monitoring and accountability.

This model also allows a correlation and comparison with structures. School structures are subject to change – for example, the changes in teachers' conditions of service brought about by the workforce reform National Agreement have altered the relationships between groups of workers in schools. There was a time when the head's secretary, caretaker and cook were the principal non-teaching roles – such staff were very much in the minority in a school staffroom. Today, in many secondary schools the number of support staff closely matches the number of teaching staff (when site, catering, administrative, technical and financial staff are counted), so creating an imperative for change.

———— References ————

Ball, Stephen, J. (1987) *The Micro-politics of the School: Towards a Theory of School Organization*, Methuen, London.

Croner, *Teachers' Rights, Duties and Responsibilities* 5th edition by Chris Lowe, CCH Group, London.

Fullan, M. (1993) *Change Forces: Probing the Depths of Educational Reform*, Falmer Press, London.

Stoll, L., MacBeath, J., Smith, I. and Robertson, P. (2001) 'The change equation' in MacBeath, J. and Mortimore, P. (eds) *Improving School Effectiveness*, Open University Press, Buckingham.

chapter five

Headteacher performance management

Making headteacher performance management work

The school improvement partner

Objective setting

Monitoring the objectives

Conclusion

The performance management system is built upon the line management structure. Inevitably this causes something of a difficulty when it comes to the headteacher, since there really is no line manager for this role. The Education (School Teacher Appraisal) Regulations 1991 determined that the arrangements for headteacher appraisal were that the local education authority (LEA) should, in consultation with governors, appoint two appraisers for the headteacher, at least one of whom would be someone who is, or has been employed as, the headteacher of another school within the same phase as the head to be appraised. The other appraiser would probably be the link adviser for the school, although this was not determined in the statute. There are a couple of important points to consider here. First, the head would end up being appraised by someone who is a peer (i.e. the most likely arrangement was that heads of other schools within the authority would provide the appraisers) and someone else who has only a glancing knowledge of the work of the head (i.e. the link adviser). Second, although there is no line of accountability from the head to the LEA (the LEA is not the head's line manager), these regulations gave the LEA the biggest say in the appraisal arrangements.

Of course the 1991 regulations were a product of their time. We have already discussed some weaknesses of the system in Chapter 1. With the headteacher version of appraisal in the same regulations we seem to have a system that virtually institutionalised cosiness and lack of challenge. It is not hard to imagine the situation that would transpire. A headteacher is identified as a peer appraiser for a colleague within the local authority. This is likely to be someone the head knows well, and furthermore is someone for whom there is no accountability for the outcome. It would therefore seem to be very much in the appraiser's interests to provide the colleague with a good review and move on. Of course the link adviser, or other LEA nominee, would be in the loop too, and this may have been sufficient to introduce an appropriate level of challenge to the process, but given there is no accountability relationship between the link adviser and the head, then even if the adviser is able to provide a sharply focused appraisal, the head does not really have to take much notice of the appraisal.

For these reasons the case for updating the appraisal procedures for heads was, if anything, even more pressing than for other teachers. The new performance management arrangements for heads introduced in the 2000 regulations for the first time placed governors at the heart of the process. Under these regulations governors have responsibility for reviewing the headteacher's performance and for setting objectives for the headteacher. During the performance management cycle governors are responsible for monitoring progress towards the objectives set, and at the end of the cycle governors then review progress towards objectives and determine whether or not a performance-related pay rise up the leader-ship spine is merited.

Clearly this process represents a significant shift into the professional arena for governors who, for the most part, are appointed or elected sub-stantially on the basis of their lay credentials. And indeed the only gov-ernors who by their nature have professional knowledge and experience, the staff governors are (rightly) specifically excluded from taking part in the process. To tackle this problem, the 2000 regulations required the intro-duction of a governors' external adviser (EA). The resulting system then gave the responsibility for headteachers' performance management to governors, but provided them with disinterested advice from a profes-sional adviser. This new performance management system represented a substantial shift from the previous arrangements. While the EA might be regarded as in some way equivalent to the appraisers under the old system, in one substantial respect there is a difference – and that is in terms of accountability. It is quite clear that the EA's responsibility is to advise the governors in their best interests – there is no cosiness in the relationship. To remove any risk of such a relationship developing, the EA is excluded from acting with a particular school for more than three years.

Making headteacher performance management work

The first part of the process of headteacher performance management is for the governors to decide upon a panel of at least two governors to act as the performance review panel. Governors are free to decide how to go about this, they should consider their decisions carefully. They need to be very aware that this is a potential point of friction in their relation-ship with the head and therefore need to be sensitive when making their selection. In short, we do not advise governors to make the selection based simply upon who happens to be on a particular committee (staffing usu-ally), or on who volunteers first. The critical factors in governor selection for this committee are that governors selected should:

- understand the process;
- understand the context of the school;
- understand the priorities of the school;

- have no 'agenda' to pursue with the head on any matter, this is not a time for settling scores;
- be prepared to put the necessary time in to monitor the process and to provide the written reports according to the timescales required.

Having put together a committee to carry out the performance management process, the governors then select an EA. The contract for managing the process of headteacher performance management nationally has rested with Cambridge Education Associates (CEA). Their responsibility is to train EAs, to provide governors with a database from which to choose an EA and to monitor and manage the process through the provision of the necessary paperwork and by ensuring that the process is carried out according to predetermined timescales. CEA will therefore provide heads and governors with prompts about what to do when within the process and ensure that EAs are allocated and carry out their work. The provision of EAs is a costly matter: for preparation of initial reports, carrying out visits and following up, the time allocation is two days, which will be charged at around £500 per day, or £1000 per school. With 23,000 maintained schools in England, then simple arithmetic shows the process costs £23 million just for the adviser time – and this is before the back office functions provided by CEA are accounted for. These costs are borne by central government, which controls the contract with CEA, thus demonstrating a considerable commitment to the process.

The EA's role then is to provide guidance for governors on how to evaluate the performance of their headteacher and to suggest suitable objectives. The basis of the evaluation is a desk study of documents provided for the EA by the governors (though the reality is, of course, that it is the head who provides the documents). The EA would expect to be provided with a copy of the school improvement plan, the school's own results analysis and the current Performance and Assessment Report (PANDA). They would also review any recent Section 10 inspection report, or any other material that was available. As we move into the New Relationship with Schools, then the EA would also expect to have access to the school's self-evaluation form (SEF). CEA provides heads with forms to carry out a self-review; here the head would be expected to describe progress towards the previously set objectives under the headings of leadership and management, pupils' progress and any other objectives that were set. The head should also carry out a general performance self-review.

It is important that the EA receives the evidence base for the performance review at an early opportunity so that it may receive appropriate consideration. The EA will then carry out an analysis of the evidence and create a commentary upon which the performance review may initially be based. The EA will arrange to meet with the headteacher alone, in order to clarify any issues and to discuss the initial findings of the analysis. Then the governors meet the EA alone. The purpose of this meeting is for the EA to assist the governors in achieving a measured view of the performance of the head and to give them the opportunity to consider a wider range of dimensions of performance than they may do left to themselves. In essence the EA ensures that the governors carry out their role of challenging and supporting the head appropriately. The emphasis on challenge is because there can be an element of cosiness in the relationship between head and governors. The emphasis upon support is because it can equally be the case that governors may not sufficiently appreciate the pressures the head experiences and they can, on occasion, present a somewhat negative perspective towards the head, seemingly never satisfied with anything that is done. The EA will also discuss with governors how they might go about monitoring progress throughout the year – because, just with performance management in the rest of the school, performance management must be an ongoing process, not a one-off event.

The final aspect of the school visit is a meeting between the head, governors and EA. At this point the governors should have been sufficiently primed to carry out the meeting without significant intervention from the EA – this is a subtle but important point as it is the governors who carry out the performance review and not the EA.

Having concluded the performance review the information can then be fed into the salary review, which may be carried out by the same committee (the approach we would advise), or by a different remuneration committee. Salary review is not the subject of this book, but it is appropriate to observe that the arrangements surrounding headteachers' pay are complex and change frequently – but they are very important to headteachers! It would not be appropriate to withhold progression along the pay spine simply for financial reasons: if the performance of the head merits a pay rise within the guidance of the current School Teachers Pay and Conditions Document (STPCD), then a pay rise should be awarded.

The school improvement partner

The DfES under the Labour government of 2001–5 came to the view that for schools to make further progress then there needed to be a new, more trusting relationship between government and schools. Broadly, the aim of this New Relationship with Schools, as expressed by Ruth Kelly (Secretary of State for Education) and David Bell (HMCI), was: '. . . to help schools raise standards – with clearer priorities, less clutter, intelligent accountability and a bigger role for school leaders in system-wide reform'. Some of the key features in the New Relationship are shorter inspections with far fewer inspectors, with the brief to quality-assure the school's own self-evaluation and – most importantly – the introduction of what has been termed a 'single conversation' with an accredited school improvement partner (SIP). The notion of the single conversation is not so much that schools would only have to have one conversation in the year, but rather that the multiple demands placed on schools could be channelled through one contact – the SIP. Who would the SIP be? For secondary schools there is an expectation that 75 per cent of SIPs would be serving headteachers or those with very recent headship experience, the remainder being comprised of link advisers or independent consultants. Currently the picture for primary schools is less clear: there is an expectation that some primary SIPs will be serving heads, but the likelihood is that a much larger proportion will be local authority link advisers.

In practice this means that the key conversations heads have with external agencies are with their link adviser, who will fulfil the local authorities' functions for monitoring, challenge and support for schools, and performance management with the external adviser. Moreover, in the spirit of the single conversation, it becomes necessary for headteacher performance management to be carried out by the SIP rather than by an additionally appointed EA.

However, there is a slight difficulty in principle here, because the EA works for the governors to advise them on headteacher performance management, while SIPs work for the local authority. The independence and confidentiality of the work of the EA is of critical importance to both heads and governors, so if SIPs are to provide this function then this must be taken into account. On the other hand there is a very great advantage with the new arrangements. This is that whereas the EA is someone who visits the school once a year, probably getting no further than the head's office, and must base his or her judgements entirely upon the documents provided and conversations with the head and governors, the SIP is someone who has a much more significant relationship with the school with an allocation of, typically, three days in school and two days in preparation. The consequence of this is that the advice provided to governors by the SIP will be more detailed and based upon a much more thorough knowledge of the school and the head – which can only benefit all concerned in the process.

Objective setting

Whether you are the head who is being performance-managed, or the governors who are carrying out the performance management, the question of objectives is particularly vexed. In particular, the nature of objectives is constrained: there must be one objective relating to pupil performance, one for leadership and management, and then there is the option of a further objective frequently relating to the headteacher's own professional development. The number of objectives to be set has been the cause of significant debate between employers and teacher unions. The broad view from the union side of the debate is characterised by the NASUWT model policy on performance management (2001), which 'provides for only three objectives to be set for each individual teacher, rather than allowing the excessive or unlimited numbers proposed in other models'. While there is undoubtedly much to commend this point of view, it means there is a limit to the extent to which the performance management process can reflect all the priorities the headteacher may have, or indeed those that the head and governors might wish for. The risk is that the agreed objectives may come to form only part of the agenda for the year rather than reflect the true objective of the school. Indeed, this can be compounded by the desire (and indeed advisability) to make the objectives highly specific.

At the most basic level, governors would wish for the head to lead and manage the school well and for all pupils to do as well as they possibly can. The question is, to what extent this broad objective is realised if the objectives set for the head of a 1400-pupil 11–18 school are, for example:

- to achieve 48 per cent five A*–C grades;

- to implement the agreed teaching and learning responsibilities (TLR) restructuring;

- to become accredited as a school improvement partner.

These objectives are certainly important outcomes for the school – they are appropriately large scale, have a whole-school impact, and there is a professional development objective from which the head would certainly benefit – but are the governors really saying that this is all they expect the head to achieve in the year? Do the results for 14-year-olds really not matter? What about A-level results? What about the whole range of other aspects of leadership and management that are about 'keeping the show on the road' rather than developing new things?

Governors and heads devising objectives will know the priorities for their own schools, and if they are unsure then they have an EA or SIP to help them, but for performance management to have any meaning at all then it is our view that objectives should be carefully crafted to reflect the whole range of the work of the school. How easy this is to achieve depends to a degree upon the systems and structures already set up in the school. We recommend a set of key outcomes for the school; the objectives can then be to achieve those key outcomes. There should also be a school improvement plan that identifies and plans for the achievement of the key improvement priorities for the school (obvious but still not in place in every school), and then one objective will be to complete the school improvement plan.

Of course, it is highly unlikely that the head will achieve the objectives set – or if they do then we would have to question how challenging the key outcomes and the school improvement plan were – so this means that there needs to be a more sophisticated approach to judging the performance of the head. And this is exactly how it should be: leading a school is a complex, sophisticated and subtle business and so the tools used to measure performance must be equally subtle. Setting a complex, non-straightforward but nonetheless specific series of objectives as suggested has to be the way forward, but not interpreting those complex objectives in a simple and unsophisticated way has to be the corollary.

Using data to set objectives

A key tool in the armoury of the EA, or the SIP, is the dataset that is provided and the analysis that this dataset enables. We have moved a very long way from the highly simplistic PANDA with its grades based upon performance in similar schools (where similar is defined solely in terms of the proportion of pupils entitled to free school meals). Over the last few years the data available to evaluate school performance has become increasingly sophisticated. The Fischer Family Trust (FFT) provides analyses of school performance and projected performance based upon a basket of measures. Key among these is the prior attainment baseline – i.e. performance in key stage national tests. The dataset also takes into account a whole range of other factors – including gender, ethnic origin of the pupil, whether or not they are entitled to free school meals and the stage on the Special Educational Needs (SEN) Code of Practice (no special need, school action, action plus or statement) – thus producing a measure of whether or not pupils in one school perform as well, better or less well than other similar pupils across the country. The FFT takes this one step further and recognises that pupil performance also depends upon the nature of the school in which the pupil is studying, and so the analysis is also able to identify how well pupils attain in a particular school compared to how they might have performed in similar schools elsewhere in the country. A further step is what is known as the FFT PANDA supplement, which provides information about trends in a school over a three-year period for the whole school and for each of the groups identified (i.e. prior attainment bands, gender, SEN, ethnic group and so on). Importantly for objective-setting purposes, this report also provides an indication of how a school might be expected to perform in future years based upon its trends over the previous three years. These trend indications are very valuable for populating the performance indicator grid for the school.

In the future it is likely that the various agencies (Ofsted, DfES) will come to an agreement on a common dataset for contextual value-added (as it is known), thus making matters considerably more straightforward than they are at present with the various approaches competing with one another. It is also likely that the secondary school data will provide information at the level of individual subjects rather than just for English, mathematics and science and threshold measures at GCSE. Clearly this information will be immensely useful to school leadership teams up and down the country.

What is the impact of all of this data on objectives? The analysis identifies specific subject areas and specific groups of pupils where there is underachievement. Would it be appropriate then to set an objective, for example, to improve the performance of middle-ability boys in English? Or the performance of children entitled to free school meals in mathematics? Or even performance overall in French? If these are significant areas of underperformance then they become priority areas for action and therefore would be admirably suited to the creation of performance objectives for the head. But this brings us back to the argument about specific objective setting. If the head has three (or possibly four) objectives that should define their work over the coming year and if one of those is to raise the performance of middle-ability girls in English, then where does this leave the rest of the school? It seems to us that it is entirely appropriate to set a broad basket of attainment objectives as already indicated, but when it comes to specific department performance this should be subsumed within those whole-school targets. Simply put, the subject-specific objectives belong to the heads of those subjects and the teachers within those departments. Setting subject-specific objectives for the head runs the real risk of distorting the priorities of the school.

Monitoring the objectives

Just as with performance management for other staff, it is not acceptable to review headteacher performance only once a year at the performance review meeting. It is vital that monitoring should take place on an ongoing basis. Indeed the monitoring procedures are something that the EA will wish to discuss with both governors and the head during the review meeting. How should this be achieved? Of course the problem with monitoring is so often that it becomes a paper-driven exercise that creates a bureaucracy all of its own, but at the same time governors do need to satisfy themselves that matters are being progressed – so monitoring procedures need to be able to square this particular circle.

CASE STUDY 1

The underachieving school

Mark was a new head in an underachieving school. The reason for underachievement was substantially poor leadership and management from Mark's predecessor. As a result of this lack of direction, Mark inherited a governing body with low expectations of their headteacher and a relatively high level of mistrust. The governors had begun to see themselves as the only solution to the difficulties the school was facing and had started interfering in the operations of the school, even to the extent of drawing up a school improvement plan in the absence of the head. At an intellectual level the governors realised that this was not appropriate, and they were also pleased that Mark, their new appointment, was able to articulate a clear vision for the school and was also evidently possessed of the leadership qualities to achieve that vision. Nonetheless, the governors were not emotionally ready during Mark's first year to give him the trust he needed. One of Mark's first steps was to encourage governors to engage an EA and to set him some objectives. These were to:

■ create a leadership structure to fulfil the school priorities for raising achievement;

- present options for governors to restructure the committee and recast the terms of reference to achieve the strategic priorities of the school;
- create a strategic plan to raise achievement;
- aim for 50 per cent of year 11 cohort to achieve five A*–C grades.

Given the predicament of the school and the need to recast the leadership, and also given the very perilous position of GCSE attainment (particularly at the five+ A*–C threshold), then these were objectives that definitely identified the core activity that both Mark and the governors would want for his first year. Mark's position with the governors was quite tricky as a consequence of their immediate history and experience of dealing with Mark's predecessor, so he encouraged them to take a very active role in monitoring his progress towards these objectives. He set up a series of meetings with the performance management committee and presented them with a review of progress towards the objectives to date. A copy of the monitoring paperwork for objective 1 is presented in the table below.

Objective	Success criteria	Actions	Impact
Create a leadership structure to fulfil the school priorities for raising achievement	<ul><li>The leadership structure is clear to all stakeholders and governors</li><li>All job descriptions are in place</li><li>The heads of department, heads of year and leadership team (LT) have ownership of and are held accountable for their responsibilities</li><li>Leadership effectiveness is monitored through performance management which, in turn,</li></ul>	<ul><li>Before starting at the school, held individual meetings with LT to discuss new roles</li><li>Discussed roles individually and at LT meetings</li><li>All aspects of the school's work are managed by only one member of the LT</li><li>Changed LT meetings to during school day</li><li>Produced agenda and minutes for each LT meeting</li><li>Bilateral meetings established</li><li>Created new posts of 'achievement and welfare' and business manager</li></ul>	<ul><li>LT feedback: 'feel like they are being led'</li><li>LT feedback: 'enjoy LT meetings because they are purposeful and well chaired'</li><li>LT has clearly defined roles – staff are clear who is responsible for each aspect of the school's work</li><li>Some settling in, but commitment of the LT to the new roles has led to high levels of cooperation</li></ul>

Objective	Success criteria	Actions	Impact
	is integral to the school's self-evaluation process ■ There are clear links between the structure and the school improvement plan ■ The focus of the leadership team is to raise standards of attainment	■ Gained agreement of governing body (GB) ■ Publicised to staff ■ Refurbished LT offices and redistributed LT across the site to emphasise the change and increase LT presence around the school ■ Increased capacity for change – uniform, behaviour, curriculum, personnel policies ■ Used opportunity of additional funding to bring assistant head (AH) post forward by a term ■ Set up series of activities to reinforce change of responsibilities ■ Regular meetings established between LT, and line responsibility (clear focus) discussed at bilateral meeting ■ Established each element of SIP as the responsibility of one member of the LT with clear lines of accountability ■ Used governor seminar for LT members to present their bit of the plan – emphasised change in roles to GB	■ Restructuring has identified need for particular roles ■ School is able to recruit for particular roles with a specific person specification ■ Induction programmes for new LT postholders has led to excellent progress in a short time ■ Bringing appointment of AH forward a term has increased LT capacity in a period of change ■ LT are enjoying their jobs more

There are number of important points in Mark's presentation. First, it is thorough and consequently takes the governors' desire to conduct an interim review of the head's progress seriously. Second, the objectives have been broken down into success criteria agreed at the start of the process, so consequently there is no need for dispute about what success 'looks like'. Third, the document not only indicates what actions have been taken in pursuance of the objectives, it is also evaluative – it analyses the impact of the actions taken. This last point is crucial – and yet can so easily be overlooked. We have discussed earlier the need for a sophisticated approach to the sophisticated task of performance management, and it is here that we can see this operationalised. It is not sufficient to respond to an objective by simply saying yes it has been achieved, or no it hasn't. It is equally insufficient to have a record of the activity that has gone on. Instead, the critical factor is, has it made a difference?

Mark's approach scores well both for the evaluative nature of the information supplied, and because it responds to the governors' need for reassurance. Providing governors with this sort of information gives them the essential confidence to know that the school is in safe hands.

In this case study Mark was a new head in a difficult situation. He had much to do and a governing body that was insufficiently clear about its role or its functions. Thus Mark's objectives reflected the low base from which the school was moving and the monitoring procedures reflected the way the governors needed to work with the head in these early months of their relationship. The next case study is a very different situation.

CASE STUDY 2

The successful school

Alice had been head of the school for a number of years prior to the changes in performance management arrangements. Her school had done very well: all the major indicators of performance (exam results at all levels, numbers on roll and first preferences, reputation in the community, Ofsted indicators, etc.) were all showing a very healthy move in the right direction. The governors were kept well informed of matters currently affecting the school and those that were in sight in the future. The governors always felt as though Alice was more demanding of herself than anyone else could be and so in this context found the requirement to have an EA somewhat onerous. Nevertheless this was the requirement, and so this was what they did.

The current review and objective setting process was fine. Essentially Alice agreed to her objectives, which were to meet the external exam indicators in her performance indicators and targets summary. The leadership and management objective was generally some specific task (for example, implementing workforce reform one year, or another year implementing the specialist school development plan). The governors were always fully content that they were kept well informed of developments at the school, either through reporting to committees, full governors' meetings or through the series of seminars Alice arranged prior to full governors' meetings. So when the EA started quizzing governors on their monitoring arrangements and asserting that they needed to create some monitoring process they were unsure whether this was necessary. When the EA raised the matter with Alice she was completely sure it was unnecessary. Her view was that she kept governors fully appraised of the progress of the school and that introducing additional monitoring arrangements specifically for her performance management was a completely unnecessary addition to her workload.

There is a real contrast in these two case studies between heads in different contexts. We would support each approach given the context. This is because both were based on a clear understanding of the relationship between the head and the governors at that particular time, and both were based on an understanding of the place the school was in the improvement cycle. The key thing in determining the approach is sensitivity to the context – not hard and fast rules that ignore it.

_____ Conclusion _____

This chapter has examined how headteacher performance management has arrived at the point it is today and highlighted some of the considerations for both heads and governors as they go about the process of performance management. Unlike everyone else in the school, the head's performance management cannot be carried out by a line manager – because the head does not have one. The solution to this prior to the current performance management regulations was to organise a cosy arrangement where colleagues would review each other's performance – perhaps because governors were uncertain about whether or not they could carry out this important function. Under the new regulations governors are now placed fairly and squarely in the driver's seat of heads' performance management, but with the additional support of professional advice from an EA or a SIP. The introduction of the SIP into this role will sharpen the process considerably. This is a welcome move because, since the head's role gives them the opportunity to have the biggest impact of any individual on the school, it is therefore critically important that their performance management is seen as a lever for producing the maximum benefit. The risk is that the opportunity is lost in the vain pursuit of objectives that are too specific and of limited number: they may fit the criteria of the regulations (which demand specific and measurable objectives) but if they are not central to the task of the head they will have no impact on the school.

Reference

Kelly, Ruth and Bell, David (2005) *A New Relationship with Schools: Next Steps*, DfES.

chapter six

Looking after the support staff

What will the support staff do?

Where will the support staff work?

Managing performance

Setting and reviewing objectives

Conclusion

Teachers are salaried, support staff are hourly paid. As such support staff will be subject to Green Book conditions of service for local government services' workers (normally working up to 37 hours per week); teachers are subject to the Burgundy Book conditions of service (with 1295 hours of directed time, but needing to work to fulfil the reasonable demands of the headteacher 'as required'). Therefore while teachers are paid for the morning break at work, hourly paid staff may not be. For example, schools make decisions on how they choose to supervise students during breaktimes; most secondary schools have duty rotas that require a pro-portion of the teaching staff to undertake supervisory duties. It would be possible for the headteachers to require all teaching staff to be on duty at breaktime – provided of course that it was included in the budget for directed time. Secondary school teachers enjoy non-contact time, which is time that they use for planning preparation and assessment. (All teachers are entitled to 10 per cent of their timetabled teaching time for this purpose.) However, rarely are teachers required to account for the ways they use this time. If teachers want to spend their non-contact time reading the newspaper, then that is generally up to them. It is only when teachers have their work monitored that there is a requirement for a particular outcome during the non-contact time. Historically, teachers in most schools have considerable flexibility about when and how they work.

Why is there a difference in these conditions of service? We have to look back over the history of education to find some clues. Many early studies within the sociology of education exploited the trait model of the profession, within which teaching could be compared. A limited range of occupations with high status, such as lawyers, doctors and priests, was taken by various sociologists as being indicative of the 'true' and gener-ally accepted professions. Their common attributes were then isolated, and used as criteria against which further occupations could be judged, to assess the extent to which they approximated to the 'true' profession. Leggatt (1970) summarises the most commonly appearing characteristics:

- Practice is founded upon a base of theoretical, esoteric knowledge.
- The acquisition of knowledge requires a long period of education and socialisation.
- Practitioners are motivated by an ideal of altruistic service rather than the pursuit of material and economic gain.
- Careful control is exercised over recruitment, training, certification and standards of practice.

■ The colleague group is well organised and has disciplinary powers to enforce a code of ethical practice.

The history of schoolmasters of the oldest public schools is one of scholastic tradition, where the decision making for the curriculum rested firmly in the hands of the individual. Schoolmasters needed non-contact time to pursue their scholarship. The tradition of secondary school teachers in many ways follow that tradition. While the political and sociological construct of the job of a teacher has changed, few would argue the necessity for teachers to have non-contact time to prepare, plan and assess.

Once we accept the need to have a new cadre of staff to undertake the range of tasks previously tackled by the teaching staff, a number of key questions emerge. What will the support staff do? Where will they work? What is the interface between the support staff and the teaching staff? Who will manage the performance of support staff? What will be appropriate objectives for them and how will these be reviewed? It is these questions that we must address.

The question of what support staff will do is perhaps more problematic than may first appear. Some issues are revealed in this first case study.

CASE STUDY 1

Heads of year

Masterton School is a successful 11–18 comprehensive with 1200 children. The pastoral structure is a traditional one. Each year group is led by a head of year who historically has been remunerated with three management points and will eventually receive a TLR2 payment. Three of the heads of year have their own office; the other two share. There is no regular administrative support. Heads of year receive a timetabled teaching remission of five periods per cycle. Typically heads of year at Masterton School will investigate disciplinary issues that occur, and lead the tutor team. They take on the year group when the children are in year 7, and take them through the school until the end of year 11.

The costs of the five people doing the heads of year job is about £75,000 (this is an allowance for each person, the timetable remission and the ongoing costs, but does not include the office space and associated administration costs).

One of the heads of year is retiring this year and another has said he doesn't want to do the job any more. Typically Masterton School has had difficulty recruiting people to heads of year posts and there is a concern that there will not be many who apply if the current structure is maintained.

The leadership team decides that it would like to review and remodel the way in which this aspect of the school is managed.

The issues in this case study reflect many of the challenges associated with the management of the tutorial or pastoral system – although they could equally apply to the management of subjects and other areas. The costs are considerable for the current structure; it is a job that few people at the school want to do; and there is no administrative support and so this means that the postholders have to do their own. In addition, the job is not focused on teaching and learning, and so there is an issue about whether a teacher is best placed to do it.

The key questions we raised earlier – and highlighted by this case study – cannot be considered in isolation, as they form part of a connected challenge, but we will take them in turn to make the issues easier to address.

_____ What will the support staff do? _____

To answer this question fully we need to decide what it is that makes a teacher's job. What is it that goes on in schools that requires a trained teacher? Is it the multitude of tasks that are undertaken in schools every day? If so, is it important that a teacher does it, do they need to do more of it and what are the barriers to this happening?

CASE STUDY 2

A problem for the class teacher

A telephone call is received at the school office. Tristan is refusing to do as the head of geography has told him. He is being disruptive in class and he is affecting the progress of the rest of the class.

Tristan's head of year goes to the lesson and Tristan leaves with him.

What happens next?

This case study illustrates many of the questions we need to consider when debating what makes a teacher. In this case the student is refusing to comply with the teacher and is preventing the learning of others – he needs to be dealt with and the neutral act (or punitive, if this is how it is seen) of removing him from the scene is the critical act. Does it need to be a teacher who removes him from the scene? Of course, we might say that he goes with the head of year simply by virtue of the power and authority of the postholder. Perhaps this is exactly the point: power and authority in this scenario is about the position in the organisation and not about being a teacher. Would Tristan go with anyone who had the authority to require him to do so? If the answer is yes, then it does not have to be a teacher. If the answer is no, then perhaps we need to debate if Tristan will go with anyone – he may not even go with the headteacher.

CASE STUDY 3

A problem for the head of year

Tristan is now out of his geography lesson and the head of year wants to talk to him about his behaviour. However, he has a year 10 class awaiting him. The head of year tells Tristan to sit at the back of the classroom while year 10 are taught.

During the course of the lesson, Tristan starts to get bored and mess about – he distracts other students in the class.

Tristan is now in trouble for disrupting a year 10 lesson as well as refusal to comply with the head of geography.

The head of year has been landed with a problem – Tristan has been taken out of class and arguably cannot return to lessons until the matter has been resolved. What is stopping this happening is that the head of year is teaching and is not yet available to investigate the problem and find a solution. The consequence here is further difficulty. Although the situation set out in this case study is not particularly unusual – and most schools will have systems for isolating students pending investigations – what this case study illustrates is that behaviour management systems interfere with the business of teaching and learning. In this instance, what started as someone else's problem has now become the head of year's problem and because of the demands of teaching the problem has been exacerbated.

So does it need to be a teacher who takes Tristan out of class? Does it need to be a teacher who sees to Tristan and asks him for his account of the incident? If the issue causing the difficulty is a teaching and learning one, then the head of year, as a teacher, is well placed to tackle the problem. But it is unlikely that the head of year will be in the classroom with Tristan and so the way forward still remains with the class teacher who Tristan has upset.

It is by adopting a critical and questioning approach to the work of a teacher that we are able to decide whether the tasks that teachers undertake require the professional input and training that teachers complete. Schools are human places and teachers are trained to teach – but this does not give them the monopoly or exclusivity on managing children and dealing with them.

So, if the role does not require the professional expertise of a teacher, the next step is to create a job description.

CASE STUDY 4

Juggling two roles

Masterton School's assessment coordinator, Julia, is also second in the history department. Julia organises the collection of assessment data, creating aspects in SIMS and produces lists, summaries and reports for teachers and parents. The School Information Management System (SIMS) package 'Assessment Manager' is managed by Julia. When she is asked about her two roles she says she finds them 'very difficult to juggle; coordinating and collecting all the Optical Mark Reader (OMR) sheets takes a long time, feeding them into the reader is another chore, and churning out all the sheets and copying them to teachers takes ages'.

The assessment working group has a brief to address these issues and has been given the budget for a member of the administration team to be employed.

The principle of an assessment coordinator and the jobs that are presented in this case study illustrate how roles and responsibilities have historically become part of the teacher's job, and have also grown. There are two clear questions to ask. First, what is assessment? And second, what is the assessment data? While the former is very much a discussion about teaching and learning – how children are assessed, what it means to learn, how assessment drives learning outcomes and teaching activities – the latter is more about collecting in the data, inputting the data into the management information system and creating reports. The next stage is the analysis and the action that results. We move from a professional teaching role into an administrative one and emerge in a teaching role again. What often happens is that the middle part of this – the data collection – becomes the dominant activity (because the discussions cannot take place without the data) and so the teaching and learning task is subsumed into an administrative one.

The job description in Table 6.1 was drawn up to identify the main purposes of the job that was to be responsible for the 'administration of all aspects of assessment and reporting, and other administration duties as required in support of the leadership team and heads of department'. The reporting lines were clearly identified and this freed up the assessment coordinator role (a teacher) to focus on the 'how' of the assessment and the analysis, because the collection of data was covered in the administration role.

TABLE 6.1   Sample job description for assessment administrator

Key tasks:

1 Assessment data:

- To be responsible for the maintenance of the SIMS Assessment Manager module: this will involve entering and checking data on pupils and will include producing tables of data for the teaching staff, reports, etc.
- To assist the assessment coordinator by producing data summaries, for example comparing actual grades with predicted grades.

2 Student reports:

- To produce the report sheets for staff as per the assessment calendar: this will involve collecting student data in advance and pre-populating the student reports with attendance, assessment and curriculum information.
- To collect the attainment group information, grades, exam results, etc., as set out in the assessment calendar, and produce reports.
- To organise the collection of student reports from staff.
- To initiate, receive and summarise reports from staff as per the assessment and reporting policy.
- To coordinate the reproduction of student reports.
- To organise the filing of reports.
- To receive and respond to parent reply slips from reports.
- To organise interim reports.

TABLE 6.1 *(cont'd)*

3 Students leaving the school:

- To organise a school leaving report for students leaving school before the age of compulsory schooling and ensure that the report is sent to the receiving school.
- To receive and circulate the reports from other schools for students entering the school during the school year.

4 Administrative role:

- To clerk the assessment reporting and curriculum (ARC) group.
- To produce the assessment calendar annually.
- To assist the examinations officer in the organisation of cognitive ability tests.
- To coordinate the production of the *Key Stage 4 Options* brochure and the yearbooks.

5 To act as a member of the administration team, assisting with duties as and when necessary.

6 Other duties as required.

_____ Where will the support staff work? _____

So, the job description has been drawn up and yet there are significant questions still to be answered. One that faces most schools is where the person will work. The burgeoning of the support staff systems in schools has created significant challenges because although a teacher may be able to do the work in a classroom, or use a satellite computer at home, employing a full-time person to do this job means providing a quality environment for them to work.

CASE STUDY 5

Location criteria

The assessment working group at Masterton School recommended that an assessment manager be appointed and drew up a job description. Julia tends to do much of the assessment work in a corner of the English faculty office. She is happy to continue to work there as it fits in with her teaching, and she is looking forward to taking on a more strategic role with assessment, working closely with the deputy head. The working group draws up a set of criteria that it thinks needs to be satisfied when identifying where the assessment manager will work. The location must:

■ have adequate space for a desk, computer and some storage;

■ be close to the rest of the administration centre so that the person feels part of the team but also can assist with team activity;

■ have a window so that there is good ventilation and be a pleasant place to work;

■ be in a separate area so that the person does not get distracted by other people's work;

■ have telephone and internet access;

■ be accessible to staff, in particular to Julia.

Managing performance

Of course, once all this is sorted out the more thorny issues of performance management come to the fore. We have discussed earlier in the book the framework for performance management of teachers. While that has its own challenges there is an even greater challenge for the support staff since often there is no framework for them at all.

CASE STUDY 6

The new recruit

Joyce has been appointed to the post of assessment manager at Masterton School and will report to Julia. Although Joyce is skilled at using Microsoft Word and Excel, she has never worked in a school. When interviewed, it was clear that she has little knowledge of such matters as levels, grades and key stages. Joyce's profile is that of an administrator in industry – which is why she has excellent ICT skills. Both her children are students of Masterton School.

The headteacher asks Julia to produce an induction programme for Joyce.

A scenario like the one in this case study is becoming increasingly common as the number of administrative staff in our schools increases. At the same time, the range of tasks they undertake grows and there is a struggle to keep up with the broad range of skills and experiences required. Teachers are inducted first of all into the profession through their training programmes. Student teachers, or interns as they are more commonly known, go on teaching practice under supervision, and consequently gain an understanding of the business of being on the staff of a school. However, support staff, particularly those who have experience gained in industry and commerce, have only their own school experience as their point of reference. There is a difference – if only because of the passage of time! Therefore the issue of induction has to be addressed and based on an assumption that the culture of the school is in many ways very different from that of the office, factory or retail environment. There are a number of issues to consider:

- *Being in a school.* As adults in school we have the responsibility for the children. Schools run to timetables: teachers have to be in their timetabled places at the appointed time and have to know where each child is at any time of the day. These factors, which those of us who are familiar with the school environment take for granted, are different from those of the office. In many workplaces, choosing when to take a break is at an individual's discretion; this is not so in a school, where activity is governed by timetables and even bells. Add to this the responsibility that we as adults in schools have for the children to ensure their safety and welfare, and we have a highly structured environment with little room for discretion. The legal framework, as well as the cultural dimension of school life, are important factors in induction of support staff.

- *The distinction between teaching and support staff.* This distinction is more evident in some schools than in others. The core activity of schools is classroom based and is led by teachers. Of course, there are many other environments where there is also a division of labour; for example, clinicians and support staff in the medical profession; or officers and civilians in the police force. However, this is an issue that faces many schools, even when they have successfully created a unified staff team. The crux of the matter is that the roles are different, so it is important to be aware of the interface between classroom life and administrative work.

- *Student management.* Staff who work in support functions may have regular dealings with students. Being clear that all staff have equal authority and equal status is essential if the opportunities presented by reform of the workforce are going to be maximised. This requires not only clarity with students and parents but also training for support staff in how to manage students. Guidance on behaviour management is essential and must be part of an induction programme, along with the more mundane tasks of writing on a whiteboard, marking an attendance register, projecting the voice, organising students to line up before going into a classroom or examination venue – the nitty-gritty tasks that experienced teachers may forget are new to support staff.

- *Jargon*. Support staff need some lexicon that enables them to engage with the jargon of education. Like most professions and industries, education has a whole range of words and phrases that are specific to our world. Getting to grips with key stages, curriculum, bands, streams, groups, GCSE, AS and A2 can be daunting. Providing guidance on this is essential for support staff.

The induction for support staff is therefore based on the practicalities of working in a school, with its legalised and highly structured environment. It is also about dealing with children, whose behaviour patterns are often different from adults. Having a detailed programme for newly appointed staff is good practice in all cases but is vital for support staff new to education.

Performance management is an all-encompassing and embracing way of working with people. It should never be something that is 'done' to people once or twice a year. Every time a line manager meets or interacts with an individual, they are managing that person's performance. This does not mean that the individual cannot act without reference to the line manager, but it does promote openness and a commitment to free and frank dialogue. This approach begins when the individual joins the organisation – literally on day one. As suggested in the case study, the assessment manager has a range of skills but is not yet fully functional in the educational setting and therefore the coaching model described in Chapter 3 comes to the fore. Information-giving and training will be fundamental dimensions of induction, but equally important will be setting targets for the first few days and weeks of the member of staff's tenure. Here the outcomes of the assessment activities for selection will be useful. In the case study, it was noted that the new member of staff was skilled with Excel but was unfamiliar with the nomenclature of grades and levels. So one target might be to produce a report for a committee – the approach should be one of direction (see Chapter 3), with the level of supervision being sufficient to ensure that the learning takes place while the task is completed.

——————— Setting and reviewing objectives ———————

Much of this discussion about support staff has been about the differences in the work of a teacher and that of support staff. As organisations grow it is likely that the overlap will be greater and increased flexibility will be needed. However, support staff are not teachers and therefore the framework we use to assess the performance of teachers is inappropriate for support staff. While for teachers we can use lesson observations, pupil progress data, subject-specific development and so on, these headings will not fit the person who, for example, is the finance officer, the receptionist or indeed the assessment manager.

We need to determine the core behaviours that we want our administration team to represent and to identify those behaviours that would represent that competence. We have identified six competencies:

■ *Communicating and influencing*. A key task for any support staff is to communicate with individuals and groups. We want our support staff to be able to communicate both written and oral information clearly and concisely. So when providing a framework for 'para-professionals', we think it is vital that they listen and ask questions to ensure understanding, and that they are able to demonstrate that understanding through their own communication methods.

■ *Continuous improvement*. One problem that is frequently associated with administration staff (and indeed in teachers who have been doing the job for a long time and who have no wish to progress on the career structure) is that of continuous improvement. If the job is not changing from one year to the next (which might be the case in some rare circumstances) how do we inculcate the principles of continuous improvement? We believe the behaviours we want to see are located first of all in the level of detail and accuracy evident in a person's work. This is because accuracy is essential in the administrative role. Furthermore, the work of the administration and support team is subject to constant change as the drive for higher standards continues, and so we need to see people who are open to new ways of working, and who were willing to share and apply good practice. A person who is committed to continuous improvement will identify and act to address their own learning and development needs.

■ *A proactive approach to meeting the needs of stakeholders*. The support staff are there to free up teachers to focus on teaching and learning – as well as to ensure that the bills are paid, that the fuel does not run out and that the business of the school is conducted. In a school the range of stakeholders is considerable, including not only the teachers and other members of the support team but also the students, parents, local employers and the community, as well as the DfES, Specialist Schools Trust, the LEA and so on. Meeting the needs of the stakeholders starts with knowing who the internal and external customers are and having a willingness to engage in the ambiguities of these relationships. When people telephone a school during a working day they expect their call to be answered in a helpful, professional way – unfortunately, this may not be a universally positive experience for callers to our schools!

■ *Planning work*. Support staff need to be able to work with a reasonable level of independence and a proportionate degree of supervision. Our corporate values are that everyone is part of the joint enterprise of providing the best quality education for the students we serve. So our support staff need to take active ownership of their work and demonstrate initiative, flexibility and a commitment to getting things done. One of the pressures that we constantly face is the need to create the resources from existing budgets – value for money in the public sector is a continuous challenge.

■ *Problem solving and judgement*. Again, there needs to be a reasonable level of independence to the way that people work and their approach to what they do. One of the questions we often ask in interviews for support staff is what they will do if they walk down the corridor and see two children squaring up for a fight. The answer is clearly not to ignore it. A good answer is to do something ranging from intervening to finding a member of the teaching staff. The ability to know when to seek help from others, understanding the remit of the job and appreciating other people's perspectives are all effective behaviours we want to see.

■ *Contributing to effective teamwork*. Most teachers are ready to collaborate to some extent. We also want this behaviour from our support staff. We don't want to see the archetypal receptionist who treats callers with disdain. We want our support staff to treat everyone with dignity and respect – reflecting our core values. Effective behaviours are those where people willingly help out others under pressure or in difficulty and will readily share the information, knowledge and skills they have.

We have collated these behaviours in Table 6.2. Our approach is to use these as the basis for the professional review where support staff are asked

TABLE 6.2   Annual review for administration personnel

Competence	Effective behaviours	Evidence
Communicating and influencing	■ Communicates written and oral information clearly and concisely ■ Listens carefully and asks questions to ensure understanding ■ Uses the most appropriate method and style of communication ■ Communicates the right information to the right people at the right time ■ Maintains the confidentiality and security of information where appropriate	
Continuous improvement	■ Pays attention to detail and ensures work is accurate ■ Identifies and acts to address own learning and development needs ■ Acknowledges own mistakes and learns from them ■ Seeks and acts upon feedback ■ Is open to new ways of working ■ Positively challenges outdated conventions and contributes ideas ■ Optimises the use of ICT ■ Identifies, shares and applies good practice	
A proactive approach to meeting the needs of stakeholders	■ Knows their internal and external customers and works with them ■ Is approachable and helpful when dealing with stakeholders ■ Acts with honesty, integrity and discretion ■ Manages stakeholders' expectations ■ Explores solutions with stakeholders ■ Meets commitments	

Planning work

- Takes ownership of work, and demonstrates initiative, flexibility and commitment to get things done
- Ensures work is planned, prioritised and delivered to meet requirements
- Is resilient and determined
- Makes best uses of resources and technology
- Successfully handles changing or conflicting priorities
- Ensures value for money

Problem solving and judgement

- Remains focused in a crisis
- Knows when to seek help from others
- Listens and takes account of diverse needs and perspectives
- Makes objective and timely decisions
- Communicates decisions to others and explains the reasons

Contributing to effective teamwork

- Treats everyone fairly and with dignity and respect
- Understands, values and incorporates others' needs, contributions and perspectives
- Builds productive and cooperative working relationships with colleagues
- Challenges behaviours and comments that undermine the concept of diversity
- Supports others by listening and encouraging
- Recognises the impact of own actions
- Willingly helps out colleagues under pressure or in difficulty
- Readily shares information, knowledge and skills with colleagues

to appraise themselves against the effective behaviours, identifying pieces of work or situations where they have demonstrated these effective behaviours. This provides the basis for discussion in a performance review meeting. By reviewing the performance of the person against the competencies, the performance issues and the areas for development emerge.

CASE STUDY 7

Reviewing performance

Joyce has been at Masterton School for six months. Julia undertakes a review of Joyce's work using the framework in Table 6.2. In the review meeting Joyce is very pleased that she has mastered the school's information management system. She recently went on some training provided by the ICT company and has seen a computerised reporting system that she thinks will significantly reduce the amount of time that teachers take writing reports and that is devoted to processing and producing the reports. Julia is keen to encourage Joyce but is worried about giving Joyce all the responsibility for introducing the new system.

In this case study, the question that Julia has to answer is whether she is worried because it is a member of the administration team who will have the expertise or whether she is concerned about the process itself. There is the additional challenge of maximising the expertise that Joyce has developed. One way forward would be for Joyce to produce a proposal under Julia's tutelage. Notice that we have moved from the directing phase to one of tutoring, because the time has surely come for Joyce to demonstrate her skills. Once the proposal has been agreed then Joyce can be supported in implementing the change. Given her level of expertise with the information management systems, the responsibility for training could also be delegated to her. This is an example of the coaching paradigm being used not only to develop a member of staff but also to empower them – allowing Joyce to make suggestions and create capacity for the future. If Julia persisted in maintaining control over the proposal, implementation, training and responsibility, then she would quickly find herself back at the stage when she was unable to act strategically because of the operational demands. Also, how would Joyce feel if her idea was taken from her?

Implementing change

It is now one year on and Joyce is implementing the change to the reports. However, at her review meeting she comments that she spends most of her time dealing with the problems raised by the programme. Julia has received complaints from members of the leadership team and heads of year that the other elements of Joyce's job are not being done.

Yet Joyce is working really hard. The reports look far better, they are of a higher quality and there have been many appreciative comments on the new reports system.

This next stage in Joyce's professional review illustrates the complexity of the change process. What started off as a job to enable Julia to focus on teaching and learning tasks has ended up with some significant management issues. Would it have been better if the reports programme had not been introduced? Perhaps it has caused more problems than it has solved, although the change has resulted in a better quality report. Technology presents us with significant opportunities, but also incredible challenges. The balancing act is one of judgement. This case study has demonstrated a school's ability to bring about change for the better – it has created capacity both with Julia and Joyce but also in the organisation as a whole. The outcome of this review might be that another member of the administration team needs to be deployed to take on some of Joyce's work to enable her to implement the change fully. It might be that the system is never sufficiently free of glitches to enable Joyce to scale down her involvement, but she may be able to train another person to work on the ICT programme and also apply the lessons she has learnt to a new context.

Conclusion

This chapter is not a celebration of support staff triumphs but more about applying the principles of coaching to the full range of experiences. By focusing on competences and behaviours, the performance management system gains a precision and clarity that enables the participants to develop opportunities within an organisation that has embraced support staff as part of the integrated whole staff team.

Reference

Leggatt, T. (1970) 'Teaching as a profession' in Jackson, J.A. (ed.) *Profession and Professionalisation*, Cambridge University Press, Cambridge.

chapter seven

Assessing progress

How to get going

What to talk about

How to keep records

The formal annual review

360-degree feedback

Working with people

Conclusion

Getting going is the first step in effective performance management relationships, but keeping going is perhaps even more challenging. It is useful at this stage to review the principles of the performance management relationship. At the beginning of this book we said that schools are very different organisations in the twenty-first century compared to 30 years ago. In some ways schools are continuing to change as organisations – for example, many of us will have been affected by the difficulties of teacher recruitment, yet in other areas of the country there is still a healthy shortlisting process for all posts. We now work in a system that is functionally based, founded on research, but moving away from the highly centralised, prescribed system of the early 1990s. The days of the individual teacher determining the curriculum for their class and how they should go about teaching it have moved through the highly prescriptive introduction of the National Curriculum and early days of the national strategies to a focus on 'how' children are taught rather than 'what'. The 'what' they are taught is directed, leaving teachers to work together on the 'how'. Teachers now work as part of extended teams where each teacher must contribute to the performance of the team as a whole and where a high priority is placed upon consistent practice and shared planning. The individual interaction between teacher and pupil is increasingly regarded as a source of potential variability. Teams have team leaders accountable for the performance and results of their team. Heads of department are leaders of teaching and learning, not administrators of resources, and as team leaders they have responsibility for managing and leading their teams.

The dominant theme of this book is that performance management is an integral part of the way in which we lead and manage. The annual statement, the summary of the annual performance review, is just that: a summary. It should never be the only occasion when two people get together to discuss one person's work. However, regular interaction and discussion about an individual's performance has to justify itself in terms of the time it takes and the likely impact.

It is to the process of performance management – the practical details – that we now turn. In this chapter we examine:

- how to get going;
- what to talk about;
- how to keep records.

Later in the chapter we will discuss the formal annual review and how we can incorporate 360-degree feedback and link the summary statement with threshold tracking and so on.

———— How to get going ————

The best way is if performance management is a whole-school initiative, but there are circumstances where a department or team might decide to develop their own approach. Indeed sometimes the 'softly softly' way can work best. The following case studies illustrate some of the issues involved.

CASE STUDY 1

Performance management at Piercy School

A recent working group on performance management at Piercy School has reported that a root and branch change is needed to the way things are done. The current system isn't working. At the moment each teacher writes their own review statement – it is very difficult to keep a check on which has been completed, the review statements lack any rigour and there is no consistency of approach. The head of Piercy School, Dean, and his deputy, Louise, think that aligning the performance management cycle to the school improvement planning cycle is one way forward. They agree that line managers should lead on performance management but are concerned that heads of department and heads of year will resist the increase in workload. They also fear that people will feel disenfranchised because performance management will definitely become something that is 'done to them'.

There is a heads of department meeting next week and this could be a useful occasion to air some of these issues.

The opening chapters of this book have discussed how to develop a performance management policy. This case study identifies some of the issues that can arise and also emphasises the benefits of a working group if major change is going to take place. Having a working group enables the issues to be aired, discussions to take place and objections managed. The issue here for Piercy School is not about the need for change but how the new system will be presented. Having a working group that identifies all the difficulties with the current system, and raises the implementation challenges for a new system is a useful starting point. This kind of change cannot be rushed – it needs timetabled change management and people must have the opportunity to say their piece.

Whatever system you end up with, how do you keep a check on whose review has happened and which ones are still to be done? The first stage is to think about how the cycle will operate and how it will interface with school improvement planning. The principle of performance management is that it is about the school achieving its goals, the individual's contribution to that (how else can it happen!) and individual staff development. Therefore the cycle, at whatever time of year it ends up happening, needs to be something like that set out in Fig. 7.1.

This model of performance management follows the line management structure for a school. Most importantly, the headteacher is part of the process and the head's targets are whole-school ones (for example, the five A*–C rate). The head's targets then generate targets for the leadership team. Their targets generate those of the middle leaders, which in turn inform those of classroom teachers, tutors, teaching assistants and other support staff. Of course, the target-setting process in itself does not necessarily work in this linear way – it is often a cyclical process – but the principle is that the targets are all informed and support one another. This gives rise to a process that enables some kind of timetable to be created. For example, one way of melding the school improvement plan and performance management cycle together would be the timetable in Table 7.1 on page 120.

The benefit of such an approach is that the performance review process and the school improvement planning are linked, with information from one informing the other. However, such an explicit link between the two may be a step too far for some schools and create unnecessary pressure. Performance management must be more about individual contributions to school improvement, where the evaluation processes that underpin the school improvement plan are about team outcomes.

The approach that the head and deputy in the case study need to take is to create proposals that will enable those affected by the change to be able to take the change process forward. Members of the leadership team are the ones most affected by the change proposed – it is the deputy heads, assistant heads and business manager who will have to complete the reports on the middle management team. Large departments – for example English, science, technology and mathematics – will often have seconds in departments who can do some of the review work with the rest of the team. Of course, training must be given if the task is to be completed to time and the potential of the change is to be realised.

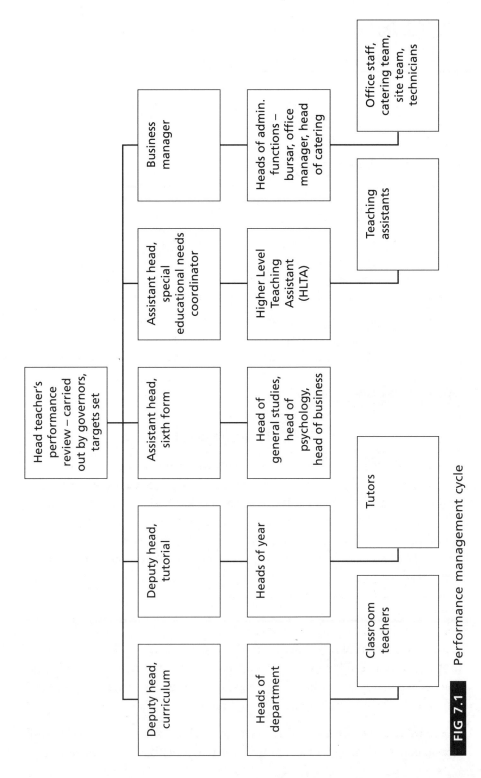

FIG 7.1 Performance management cycle

TABLE 7.1   Review and planning timetable

Month	Performance review	School improvement plan
September		Review of public examination results
October	Headteacher performance review	
November		Interim report on plan
December	Leadership team reviews	
January		Department reviews
February	Heads of department and heads of year reviews	
March		Evaluation of plan
April	All other staff reviews Headteacher interim review	
May		New plan adopted by governors
June	Leadership team interim review	Plan implementation commences
July	All other staff interim reviews	

CASE STUDY 2

The threshold issue

Dean wants the system to provide teachers with the evidence for threshold applications and also to provide him with the evidence for threshold tracking. There are a large number of staff who will be making threshold applications over the next three years and the first tranche of staff will be coming up for review next year. How can the system address the threshold issue and provide teachers with the developmental feedback they need? How will the support staff needs be addressed?

Following discussions in the working group and meetings with the leadership team, heads of department, heads of year and other staff, it is decided that performance reviews will be carried out by line managers and that teachers' reviews will follow the threshold standards format. The headings for the review statements are as follows:

- *Knowledge and understanding*. This section is about subject knowledge and also about pedagogy. Teachers may (or may not) have the relevant and appropriate subject knowledge – the starting point is the teacher's qualifications. However, there also needs to be evidence of professional updating and appropriateness of knowledge. It is not sufficient to have a first degree in a teaching subject if the teacher is not aware of recent and relevant updates to the teaching of the subject. Furthermore, there should be evidence of the teacher's subject knowledge being applied in the classroom context and further evidence of the teacher's understanding of the subject in the context of school teaching and student learning.

- *Teaching and assessment – planning lessons*. Under this heading the teacher should be able to provide evidence of planning that is tailored to the needs of students. This does not necessarily mean detailed lesson plans – the plans should be the result of collaborative planning rather than the outcome of one teacher's solitary endeavour. The critical thing is that any lesson plan shows how the scheme of work has been tailored to the needs of the individuals. The planning should also demonstrate that assessment is integrated into the way in which the lesson has been organised.

- *Teaching and assessment – classroom management*. Of course, teaching is not always about serried rows of children. The planning should demonstrate an awareness of the way in which the teaching experience will be organised to take account of the way in which the children learn (for example, reflecting the time of day, the day of the week, or how learning is structured to address the behavioural issues the class presents). This is not about controlling children but about structuring the teaching to ensure that learning is maximised.

- *Teaching and assessment – monitoring progress*. There are the times when the progress of the pupils is summarised. However, the good teacher has ongoing methods of monitoring the progress of the pupils in the class. This means marking and assessment (as evidenced by classwork, homework, and projects and testing). Teachers should be able to provide some form of record of the work that has been set and assessed.

- *Pupil progress*. This is the place where the teacher is able to demonstrate the progress that pupils make as a result of the teaching. The point is not the evidence of analysis (i.e. lots of lovely graphs and charts) but that the teacher demonstrates an awareness of target grades and evaluates the teaching in terms of progress against the targets. The reference should be both historical and current.

- *Wider professional effectiveness – personal development*. The expectation should be that teachers are developing personally – this is the responsibility of the individual, with support from the school.

- *Wider professional effectiveness – school development*. What has been the teacher's contribution to whole-school development? At head of department level this might include department self-evaluation and department development planning. Every teacher needs to demonstrate a contribution to the development of the school.

- *Professional characteristics*. This can be quite difficult to evaluate. One way is to use the National Standards, which for heads of department is:

  - strategic direction and development of the subject;
  - teaching and learning;
  - leading and managing staff;
  - efficient and effective deployment of staff and resources.

There are similar standards for mainscale teachers, providing a useful baseline for evaluating professional standards and characteristics. However, the National Standards model is somewhat functionally based and rather deterministic. Effectiveness is not just about 'doing the job' in the sense that the required tasks are completed to a certain standard. The following professional characteristics were drawn up by Hay McBer for school leadership, but are applicable to many different roles:

- Analytical thinking: the ability to think logically, break things down and recognise cause and effect;

- Challenge and support: a commitment to do everything possible for each pupil and to enable all pupils to be successful;

- Confidence: a real belief in one's ability to be effective and to take on challenges;

- Developing potential: the drive to develop others' capabilities and help them realise their full potential;

- Drive for improvement: relentless energy for setting and meeting challenging targets, for pupils and the school;

- Holding people accountable: the drive and ability to set clear expectations and parameters and to hold others accountable for performance;

- Impact and influence: the ability and the drive to produce positive outcomes by impressing and influencing others;

- Information seeking: a drive to find out more and get to the heart of things, intellectual curiosity;

- Initiative: the drive to act now to anticipate and pre-empt events;

- Integrity: being consistent and fair, keeping one's word;

- Personal convictions: a passionate commitment to education, based on deeply held values and beliefs, or born out of a desire to serve pupils, parents and the community;

- Respect for others: an underlying belief that individuals matter, and deserve respect;

- Strategic thinking: the ability to see patterns and make links, even when there is a lot of detail, and to see the big picture;

- Teamworking: the ability to work with others to achieve shared goals;

- Transformational leadership: the drive and the ability to take the role of leader, provide clear direction, and enthuse and motivate others;

- Understanding the environment: the ability to understand and make positive use of the relationships or social and cultural differences with the school or in organisations in the wider community;

- Understanding others: the drive and an ability to understand others, and appreciate why they behave as they do.

This is quite a long list and certainly a school embarking on a new performance management system needs to think carefully about which tools it uses to enable people to evaluate their own and others' performance. The balance that has to be struck is having sufficient tools to shape a review but not to make it into some kind of extended tick list or exhausting process. The school in our case study decides that it is going to use the threshold standards as the headings for the performance review and keep the Hay McBer characteristics as a resource for development in the future.

_____ What to talk about _____

The school now wants to provide training for the staff and to develop systems so that it all happens, with the opportunity to address any emerging problems.

The geography department

Simon joined Piercy School 18 years ago as head of geography. Geography is improving at GCSE, but at A level, although it recruits well, the results are weak and the head has asked Simon to draw up an action plan. Simon has produced the plan and now Louise, the deputy head, wants to meet with him to discuss it.

At the heads of department meeting Simon supported the introduction of the new performance management system. He now has to set up meetings with members of his team: Robyn and Steve. Robyn is in her third year of teaching and she is a very good teacher, although she struggled during her induction year. Simon spent a lot of time in that first year supporting her with her classes – now they still talk often but it's mainly about naughty pupils.

Steve has been teaching geography at Piercy School for 20 years and rarely needs any support from Simon. They are very good friends and live in the same village – they sometimes come to work together. They have daughters of the same age who play together. Steve's results have been fine but have not kept pace with the school improvement that has occurred during Dean's headship.

As the same time, Simon has to prepare for his first review meeting with Louise.

There are a number of issues to address in this case study and they underline the need for training and staff development. The first thing that Louise needs to do is set up a meeting with Simon. The aim of the meeting must be that Simon is guided through the performance review process: the discussion can be used to model the ones that Simon will hold and give him the opportunity to share any concerns. By the end of the meeting Simon needs to have a clear idea of what he has to do and be appropriately skilled to hold the first meetings with Robyn and Steve.

We believe that whenever people are asked to attend a meeting they should know what it is for and what is to be discussed. When the meeting represents a change in practice then some will be anxious and may worry about what will happen and what will be expected of them. So, some form of agenda is desirable. By publishing the agenda in advance it is clear to the head of department what the meeting will be about: it is about results, it is about staff performance and also it is about the leadership of the department. So when this meeting takes place a discussion about each of these will be anticipated. By preparing for the meeting, the line manager (in this case Louise) can also respond to any queries or objections that the head of department has.

Louise asks Simon to prepare for the meeting by providing her with the information on the department. She chooses to do this because it suggests that the meeting is a joint one (rather than something that is going to be 'done' to the head of department) and also that there is an expectation that meetings are planned. By doing some preparation herself and also requiring Simon to do some research, the meeting assumes a more professional status and locates the interactions in the context of school improvement.

CASE STUDY 4

Agenda for the first meeting with the head of department

- Department statistics over the past three years.
- Profile of the department – strengths and weaknesses.
- How the department is faring with the current GCSE target.
- Department issues over the next two years.
- How the head of department is managing the situation – relationship with each member of the team.
- Progress with the school improvement plan.

The meeting with Simon has to fulfil three functions:

- to review the action plan he has produced;
- to prepare Steve for the first professional review meetings;
- to enable him to hold similar meetings with Steve and Robyn.

CASE STUDY 5

Meeting with the head of department

Louise is concerned about the action plan because it is insufficiently focused on strategies to bring about improvement: the actions that Simon has suggested are mostly about going on external courses and there will not be a review of progress until the mock exams in January. Louise thinks that she needs to challenge Simon about this – she wants to develop his analytical skills so that he uses data to target interventions. Although the GCSE scheme of work is completed, the A-level scheme of work is only in draft outline form and in the course of the meeting it becomes clear that Simon has not observed any sixth-form lessons and that sixth-form teaching is rarely a subject for department meeting discussion. The entire meeting between Simon and Louise is given over to the discussion of the action plan and so there is no progress on the performance management issues. However, they have agreed to meet the following week and so Louise summarises the meeting in a memo:

To: Simon Begley

From: Louise Reed

Date: 24 August 2005

Re: A level geography

Thank you for the action plan you sent to me. At our meeting today we discussed the plan. We agreed that there are a few more details that show me exactly how you are going to bring about the required improvement and the detailed steps you are going to take. I would be grateful if you could add these to your action plan, using the strategies you have already identified as follows:

- *summary of key issues from 2004–5 (you might want to refer to examiner's reports from previous years);*
- *targets for 2006 (you might compare the year 12 exam grades with the target grades to deduce the extent of the task; also, please analyse the GCSE grades for year 12 to assess the outcome for AS);*
- *step-by-step action plan, in tabular form (I showed you one that the biology department produced last year – I know that Nigel would be pleased to discuss how his worked out);*
- *involvement outside the department (for example, head of sixth form, geography adviser?).*

I look forward to meeting with you next week to progress the plan further.

The memo from Louise has been used to record the outcomes of the meeting and sets down what has been agreed. Depending on the culture of the school, the reaction to such a memo may vary from the benign (or even someone thanking you for doing the aide-memoire) to the reactive. Some people may regard the memo as a threatening document – we know of teachers who have been concerned that this is the first stage in some form of disciplinary process! In this case study the memo is simply a way to record the meeting and help Louise to remember what has been agreed and Simon to be clear about what he is to do. By summarising the meeting in this form, Louise is saying that the meeting matters, it is worthy of recording and, furthermore, the she expects the agreed actions to be progressed by the next meeting. Although the memo is not the sword of Damocles, if the next meeting starts without any progress on the action plan, it gives rise to a conversation about how the work is going to progress.

CASE STUDY 6

Developing a dialogue

At the next meeting Louise and Simon review the action plan and it is more specific in terms of actions and analysis. However, there is very little on sixth-form schemes of work. Simon agrees that the results are not good enough, but resists the idea of a detailed scheme of work for A level and says it is not necessary because the staff know what they are doing. During the course of the meeting, Louise and Simon engage in a very long discussion about the function of schemes of work and the role of the head of department in monitoring the teachers in the department.

Would this conversation between Louise and Simon have happened had the meeting not have been convened? Having the meeting and focusing on school improvement creates an agenda where two colleagues can discuss issues – regular dialogue is always better than a sporadic meeting to discuss a particular matter. What the deputy head in this case study has done is to model the process of performance management for Simon. There is an agenda focused around what the person is doing – the discussion starts off as a meeting about a task, but develops through the agendas of action plans, data analysis, curriculum planning and monitoring. Through this Louise is able to show Simon in a practical and demonstrative way how to tackle issues and raise the expectation of forward development.

How to keep records

As we illustrated, one way to keep records is to follow each meeting up with a brief memo summarising the main points of the discussion and recording the action points for the following meeting. There are a number of benefits from this approach:

- it shows the colleague that this meeting matters – it matters so much that you are spending your time recording the outcome;
- it will enable them to remember the action points for the next meeting (if staff feel threatened by this then tell them that the memo is to help you to keep track, etc.);
- it forms a cumulative record of the person's work over time, so when it comes to undertaking a review of the person's work then there is a body of information that can be discussed and evaluated;
- it models the process of performance management – it is easier for a person to 'do this to someone' if they are having it 'done to them'.

This approach, however, is not without its difficulties – and one of them is simply keeping it going. Having a series of meetings that all need to be written up in some form does add to the workload. One answer may be to make notes during the meeting and simply photocopy the sheet for other colleagues. The sheet one team has developed together looks like the example in Table 7.2.

This approach is less formalised than the memo because the document is a joint one that is created during the meeting and so is less contentious. Of course, writing things down in this way might inhibit discussion, because some time will need to be devoted to recording the agreed points.

The formal annual review

Having established a working dialogue for the performance management process the next stage is the formal annual review. One element of this is the lesson judgement. Although we prefer the Ofsted framework, schools will have their own approaches to lesson observation. The important point at this stage to note is that it is an obligatory part of the process, but like all the elements in the performance management system it is best if it is not a once-a-year activity. Regular lesson observation will give a more realistic and accurate assessment of the strengths and areas for development of a teacher's work – judging the whole year's work on a 30-minute observation is not really fair.

We suggested that the performance review should follow the threshold standards framework – the benefit is that it enables tracking for threshold purposes and also facilitates the evidence base for portfolio assessment.

TABLE 7.2   Summary notes

Date of meeting	Summary of discussion
5 September	GCSE results were good this year in the department but there were four students in your class who didn't complete their coursework portfolios to the same standard as the rest. The first piece of work tackled in year 11 seems to be the problematic one.
	Focus for the next three weeks: make sure all the students (particularly Louise Phillips, Sam Neil and James Carr) do at least a grade C piece of work.
	Target from review: experience of budgeting.
	Prepare order for department: ready to be processed.
5 November	Year 11: worked really well. James Carr's work was grade B standard.
	Budget: recommended we bought twice as many boards because we use them quickly in term 2 – good suggestion.
	Year 8: you want to look at the scheme of work for year 8 – there's an ICT project to do and you would like to try it with your class – go for it!
	General: worried how you will cope with the mock exam marking – agreed to mark four pieces a day.
	Also you are going to see Ann to ask if you can be protected from cover as you have two year 11 groups to work with.
5 January	Preparation for review meeting. Think about the year since last January:
	1 What things have you been pleased with?
	2 What have you found challenging and how have you tackled it?
	3 Your contribution to department development.
	4 Your contribution to whole-school work.
	5 What you'd like to achieve next year.

The first stage of the performance review is to go through the objectives from the previous year. The following case studies illustrate the process.

The English department

The English department at Shuttleworth School works very well together and is noted for its collaborative approach. Bex, the head of English, agreed to a GCSE target of 75 per cent A*–C. The department worked really hard – children were regularly drafting pieces of work and the coursework was a very high standard, with 80 per cent being at least grade C and all of it above grade G.

Bex had the following objectives for the year:

- achieve 75 per cent A*–C in the June examinations;
- complete the department improvement plan;
- develop a system for lesson observation and peer observation that increases the amount of observation and is developmental;
- use the Ofsted framework to develop strategies for monitoring students' work as a whole department task.

Ed is deputy head with line responsibility for the English department, and is going to undertake the review of performance. The department finally achieved 72 per cent A*–C for English; the whole school five-A*–C rate was 65 per cent.

The challenge for this performance review is how to ensure that Bex feels that her department has done really well and still provide her with a challenge for the future. Since English is one of the most successful departments in the school and Bex is one of the best subject leaders, the challenge is considerable. The deputy head does not want Bex to feel that the department has not done a very good job. During the course of the year Ed has been sharing techniques of data analysis with Bex and she has become skilled at evaluating the department's performance. So in preparation for the meeting Ed asks her to do a residual analysis by teaching group and gender. (A residual analysis works by subtracting the grade predicted – in this case by cognitive ability tests – from the actual grade. Each grade has a points value; normally schools use A* = 8, A = 7, B = 6, C = 5 and so on. So a child with a prediction of grade C who achieves a B has a residual of 6 − 5 = 1. A child with a target of grade A who achieves grade D has a residual of 4 − 7 = −3. If the residuals are averaged for the group then a residual graph can be compiled.)

Fig. 7.2 shows what the graph looks like for English language and English literature by gender.

When Bex looks at the analysis by teaching set, the results are as Fig. 7.3.

In the discussion Bex identifies the groups of students in each teaching group who underachieved. The good residual for set 4 boys looks weaker than the girls' performance, but there were twice the number of boys in the group than girls. The areas for development are identified as boys

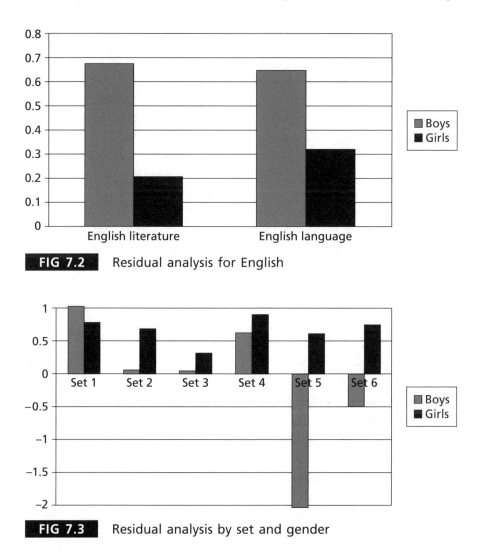

FIG 7.2   Residual analysis for English

FIG 7.3   Residual analysis by set and gender

in sets 5 and 6, both boys and girls in set 3, and boys in set 2. The analysis does not answer all the questions but it does provide a focus for discussion. In this way data analysis is being used to develop thinking about teaching and learning.

CASE STUDY 8

The review statement

The outcome of this part of the discussion was a summary for the performance review:

Objectives from last year:

■ *Achieve 75 per cent A*–C in the June examinations. This was narrowly missed because the result was 72 per cent at A*–C. However, this was a challenging target and the department worked very hard to ensure that students did well. A particular feature of the way the department works is to ensure that the coursework is completed to the highest standard possible. The department works tirelessly to ensure that this happens. Bex has been looking at the way in which the creative writing assignment is being delivered. The evidence from the analysis is that the teachers in sets 2 and 3 have not managed to achieve the same standards with boys as with girls. The assignment is the same for both groups at the moment, and so Bex wants to review this with the department. In addition Bex changed the structure of the teaching so that there are two teachers instead of three – this was to help continuity and enable more focused revision work to be completed in class.*

One of the ways Bex is going to develop the department further is to make more use of revision guides, so that students will make very few notes. We discussed ways in which the guide could be interleaved so that additional information could be incorporated.

Ed and Bex go on to discuss the other objectives. The department has had a challenging year with one member of the team absent for most of the three terms. There have been things that they wanted to do but over the year Ed has supported Bex in her focus on the GCSE results. The department spent a lot of money (and this came from a successful application for curriculum development funding) on a new programme of study called 'Prose and Poetry for All'. This meant a lot of work had to be done with schemes of work, with each member of the department responsible for a section of the scheme of work. This created a heavy agenda and less time was devoted to lesson observation or work scrutiny. This is reflected in the following statements in Bex's review:

- *Complete the department improvement plan. This is on track for completion. A particular feature has been the next phase of implementation of the Prose and Poetry for All programme. This is having a big impact on teaching and learning, with high-quality materials being available. In a lesson observed with another colleague I was able to see the impact of this programme – it requires a different approach to the teaching of prose and poetry and it is already achieving its aims.*

- *Develop a system for lesson observation and peer observation that increases the amount of observation and is developmental. Some work was done on this but it is fair to say that this has not yet happened. We agreed that this is an area that needs to be reconsidered. Bex and Janey undertake lesson observation as part of performance management and induction arrangements but there is very little other lesson observation. One outcome from the January INSET day is that a calendar of observations will be produced.*

- *Use the OfSTED framework to develop strategies for monitoring students' work as a whole department task. Again, this objective has not been achieved, but it has been planned in for the remainder of the academic year. Bex has produced the calendar for the remainder of the academic year, where there are clearly identifiable slots where the work of particular year groups is to be analysed as a department activity. Clear criteria are to be developed over the next two months to enable this to happen and be beneficial.*

This review statement is sharply focused on achievement but also notes when things have not happened. The difficulty for those who carry out professional performance reviews is always how to acknowledge the teacher's good work while at the same time using the review as an opportunity to set challenges for the future. If things that are noted in the review and are set for the following year do not happen, then further conversations will need to take place, but they will be conducted on the basis of an agreed position – that these are important actions that have not been undertaken over a period of time.

This case study demonstrates how managing a member of staff who is clearly so committed and has such a command of the brief can and should be a hugely fulfilling and energising opportunity. There is the challenge, of course (as the case studies in Chapter 3 illustrate), where a person has a huge amount of raw talent and potential – working with someone of exceptional ability means that the line manager has to be ready to challenge and be challenged. There is also a challenge when reviewing underperformance, as in the next case study.

The underperformer

Joseph is head of PE. He joined the school less than a year ago as head of football and applied for the post of head of PE. He performed well at interview, although in a comparatively weak field. He has struggled to establish himself in the school – there have been quite a few student disciplinary issues. Ed, the deputy head, has been meeting with Joseph regularly and some progress has been made. However, the department's results are weak and there is significant slippage in the work the department has to do. The department self-evaluation was a poor piece of work: it's clear that Joseph has done very little lesson observation and there is no evidence of any analysis of strengths and weaknesses.

Ed has a meeting with Joseph to review his performance.

This is clearly a difficult situation because the teacher is underperforming but has had a relatively short time in post. The meeting needs to be structured in a way that brings about an appreciation of the need for higher standards. The framework for the performance review we have outlined above is a useful one to apply in this situation. The teacher has not, in this scenario, been set any objectives and therefore a formal assessment cannot be carried out, but the question on progress can still be phrased. For this meeting to move forward Ed needs to have a range of data available to discuss.

- *Data on the department.* Ed might chose to prepare data that shows the performance of the department compared with other departments. If this is broken down further by teaching group, then this will allow Joseph and Ed to look together at the way in which teaching groups are performing.

- *Data on individual students.* By looking at how students perform in PE and their other subjects, a discussion can be stimulated on the possible reasons for underperformance. Sometimes in these situations the teacher will blame the students for the poor performance, but by using comparative data it is possible to ask why students achieved well in some subjects but not in PE.

- *Evidence from lesson observations.* This is the primary evidence base, using the judgements that are being made about the quality of teaching.

- *Records from meetings*. It is in these situations that note-keeping is so important. By having records of meetings where actions were agreed there is a basis for discussion about the future direction.
- *Information from the department*. One way to develop the discussion is to ask the teacher to bring along, for example, the scheme of work for key stage 4 or examples of department development activity. By focusing on a piece of work, the discussion can be managed around the task and progressed to the leadership style.

Such meetings have the potential to be very challenging and the line manager needs to be clear about the intended outcomes. In some cases such a meeting can have far-reaching consequences about how people progress – in this case the teacher has been in post a relatively short time and this will inform the next stage. Preparing for such meetings requires considerable effort on the part of the line manager and it can be beneficial in some cases to rehearse the meeting with a colleague. On the information given, there is a need to encourage and support Joseph, but also to let him know that the department is underperforming and that significant improvements are needed.

CASE STUDY 10

Areas for development

The outcome of the meeting between Joseph and Ed is a need for more training. The following statement forms part of the review:

4.1 Wider professional effectiveness – personal development

Joseph is to participate in the middle management development course this year. He has already attended several INSET events relating to coursework, which have given him a greater understanding of the coursework standards. In addition, Joseph has had training in lesson observation from the link adviser. Joseph has carried out lesson observations of the staff, but I am concerned that the messages he is giving to the department are ones that may prevent the department from making as much progress as required. The statements in the lesson observations refer to 'excellence' when the data on the department does not support this view. The teaching cannot be excellent unless there is a corresponding excellence in the standards achieved by students. This is not the case in PE; therefore additional training will be provided during the year. Joseph has had training on performance management by me and this is developing well. He has developed systems for staff to review what they are doing and to consider the impact that this is having on student achievement; provided that this is done critically then this has the potential to have a greater impact.

This is a bluntly written performance review statement and it is a matter of judgement whether it is appropriate to phrase it in this way. However, the benefits of such a review are that the member of staff is left in no doubt that improvement is required but also that progress has been made. The areas for development emerge as:

- *Using data.* Data is required to produce summative reports but also to produce comparative reports where the performance of students is set against their results in other subjects. However, for Joseph it will not be enough to generate these reports – he will also need to ask why students in PE are underachieving while in other subjects they are succeeding. The benefit of this approach is that it moves the debate from an interpersonal one (i.e. between Ed and Joseph) to incontrovertible facts: Ed simply needs answers to the questions that the performance of students in PE is raising.

- *Lesson observation training.* The training so far has had a limited impact – regrettably Joseph has told his staff that their lessons are excellent or very good. This is all part of the debate about the relationship between teaching and learning. Can teaching be excellent if it is not reflected in results? Perhaps it is possible when a school is on an improvement strategy with a history of underachievement and some changes take a period to follow through; however, this seems less likely where the results are out of kilter with other departments. It is clear that the training Joseph has already had needs to be supported through additional input – perhaps joint lesson observation so that his judgements are moderated.

360-degree feedback

In this book we have argued strongly against the traditional approach to appraisal, even though it had the advantage of simplicity. It was a bureaucratic chore to be completed as speedily as possible: every year at the appointed time an individual would sit with their line manager (or another person) and the performance might have been discussed. In contrast, the model we have been developing is one that is continuous, flexible and revolves around dialogue and feedback. The *raison d'etre* of performance management is to improve an individual's – and therefore, an organisation's – performance. To do so, the system has to be responsive to individual needs and universally applied and available. One of the tools that has been borrowed from industry and commerce is that of 360-degree feedback. This involves the person's peers, subordinates and superordinates (and customers or clients) airing their views of the person's performance. It is not designed for the fainthearted!

The attraction of the 360-degree feedback system is that it gives a more complete picture of an individual's performance. Different groups can see an individual in a variety of circumstances and situations and can, as a result, give a broader perspective than that of one person. However, people can be incredibly sycophantic or completely negative about a person. People do not like to be negative about someone who is popular – and so there is a risk of management by popularity. Research by Ashridge Management College into the growth of 360-degree feedback (Handy et al., 1996) suggests that success requires a number of factors:

- a clear strategic rationale;
- top management support and involvement;
- a culture generally that is towards behaviours and attitudes rather than simply performance;
- sensitivity;
- a genuine and wide-based willingness to achieve change;
- willingness to discuss any issue.

This sounds quite a long list of preconditions. However, the culture can itself be developed through the use of such tools as 360-degree feedback. One thing that is non-negotiable with this sort of feedback is that you cannot expect of others what you are not prepared to do to yourself. Put simply, the best way to start a 360-degree feedback process is as an individual or a group who decides to give it a try. There are a number of options you can explore.

Student feedback

One way to start off the process as a class teacher is to ask students for feedback. This can be done in a fairly non-threatening way (but is nonetheless scary!). For example, a maths teacher had been trying out some approaches as part of the school's Assessment for Learning project. In the lessons students had been setting questions on circle theorems for other students to answer. The students were then asked the following questions:

- Which of the circle theorems did you use in your question?
- What difficulties did other students encounter with your question? How did you respond?
- How has your knowledge of circle theorems improved?
- Thinking about the way you worked on this exercise – what worked well?
- Thinking about the way you worked on this exercise – what would make it better next time?

Of course, when you ask students for their opinion you have to be prepared to do something about it if the results tell you something you do not like! However, teachers who enjoy a good relationship with their students will find that this is an affirming process that encourages them to try new things. The outcome of such an exercise (as well as informing the teaching and learning process) is one where you get used to the idea of getting feedback on what you have done.

Peer feedback

One of the less threatening ways is to introduce some form of evaluation for staff meetings or INSET sessions. By asking people for some form of feedback on the INSET session we get used the idea of seeking and receiving feedback and others get used to giving it. The example in Table 7.3 shows how this can be done.

Again, if this approach is to have any impact then the outcomes of the survey need to be shared with the staff and – of course – notice taken of them when planning further sessions.

You can also ask questions of your colleagues about your own work. This is easier if it is part of a whole-school approach, but individuals or groups can equally well adapt this process on their own. The best approach is to ask the line manager to speak to those who will be asked, to say that the responses will be shared with the individual because the person wants to improve their practice. If people do not want to contribute then their wishes should be respected.

The following case study is taken from a school that was keen to develop the 360-degree feedback approach but had not asked people for feedback in a direct way before.

TABLE 7.3   Feedback form

Please answer the following questions using the four-point scale:

1 Disagree strongly

2 Disagree

3 Agree

4 Agree strongly

Session 1: The presentation by staff on Assessment for Learning

1 The session was well organised

 1   2   3   4

2 The session stimulated my thinking on assessment

 1   2   3   4

3 The session presented me with new ideas

 1   2   3   4

4 I enjoyed the session

 1   2   3   4

CASE STUDY 11

Feedback from colleagues

Shuttleworth School has been developing its approach to performance management where there are regular meetings with individuals to discuss progress and tasks. Nigel now wants people to comment on the way he works with them. Nigel wants to know whether his approach is one that people welcome and value – he also wants to know if his style inhibits or encourages people to develop. He decides to survey the colleagues he line-manages.

The sheet produced looked like this:

1 *To what extent does Nigel provide an environment for you to develop your leadership skills?*

2 *To what extent is your relationship a collaborative one?*

3 *How does Nigel's style enable you to improve your performance?*

4 *How does Nigel demonstrate an understanding of your role?*

5 *Do you believe that Nigel is capable of developing you in your current role? If so, what has he done to help you develop? If not, please comment on what Nigel would need to do differently.*

6 *How does the implementation of the performance management system enable you to develop?*

7 *What do you gain from your meetings with Nigel?*

8 *What do you gain from lesson observations carried out by Nigel?*

9 *How do you know that your work is valued?*

10 *At this school we aim to empower all leaders to take decisions. What does Nigel do that empowers you?*

There are some far-reaching questions posed in this 360-degree feedback pro forma because the questions tackle a range of competencies. The first question focuses on the manager's ability to create an environment where the individual can develop as a leader for themselves. Tacit in this question is the presumption that the person is a leader in their own right and the question is therefore about the context in which the person works. The school has a public statement of intent that individuals should collaborate within the framework of the line structure. The questions test these out. By setting out a framework of 360-degree feedback in this way, the climate of a clear strategic rationale is sustained through action. By leading from the front – asking a group of people to comment specifically on what a leader does and the impact of those actions – there is an emphasis on behaviour and attitude as well as productivity. This approach, if sustained over time, can be a powerful force to demonstrate a willingness to discuss any issue.

Working with people

Performance management is very much about ways of working with people. Some of the structural constraints we have in our schools are a result of decisions taken by those before us – and in some cases those above us. The actions we have to take say as much about the history of the organisation as about the present.

CASE STUDY 12

Will is head of German. He has worked at the school for over 20 years. His department is very well managed. If Ed, the deputy head, goes into the German department's office he sees it is well ordered – a book, a piece of paper or document can be found very quickly. Will's department is made up of two assistant heads and the head of Spanish. Students like German – they like the well-ordered department.

However, the school was inspected last year and there were weaknesses in the department's planning. Will has always resisted having schemes of work because he says they stifle creativity: he devotes the time he has to teaching, not to administration tasks. Ed's view – which is reinforced by discussions with his leadership team colleagues – is that the imperative for planning has not been there because of having three experienced teachers in the department. So even though the subject is popular, results are not good.

Ed wants to engage Will in the debate on planning and also to raise standards in German. In addition, a new German teacher has been appointed to the school for September – she is a newly qualified teacher (NQT) and on the Fast Track programme. Will has been asked to be her subject mentor.

This case study illustrates the point that schools, like many other organisations, end up in situations that are of their own making but represent an amalgam of decisions and happenings. If the school was seeking to set up a German department it would appoint someone who was willing and able to create innovative schemes of work, devise assessment schemes, and be skilled in the use of data to bring about improvement, manage the budget and be a highly effective manager of personnel – and so on! Will may have the ability to do all of these things – he may already be doing some of them – but he is the product of his circumstances. The task for Ed is to manage this person and bring about the changes needed as part of the whole-school improvement strategy.

The difficulty Ed faces is how to bring about a change in the way that Will works. Of course the task is made more difficult because the two assistant heads have, effectively, colluded with Will. They have enabled Will to 'get away with it' because they have coped with teaching their classes without schemes of work. It is possible that they share Will's opinion on curriculum planning. Ed's approach has to be to decide what is to happen and engage in the debate. It is only through sustained discussion of the principles that any progress can be made.

The coaching paradigm we have explored enables relationships to be sustained over time. Tackling a colleague who for various reasons is not aligned with the school improvement strategy is difficult and cannot be resolved overnight. However, by assuming that it can be solved and that problems can addressed, the task becomes that much more feasible. It may be that the outcome of the meetings Ed holds with Will are that the head of German is given direct instruction on what has to be done. Of course, Will may not agree to these instructions and the recourse will eventually be a disciplinary one. However, sustained and consistent practice with all colleagues will eventually bring about an agreed position. This is organisational consistency. The levers that Ed may have to use include direct instruction, discussion, engagement of other colleagues, peer support and so on – but the approach always has to be that the person can bring about the improvement but needs the support of others to do so.

The fundamentals of an effective performance management system are that there are events that happen according to some agreed framework, that there is a requirement to discuss performance regularly and that there is a willingness to engage with people on every issue – however difficult or controversial. The last element is the most difficult because it might involve conflict; it will certainly involve setting aside any personal relationships that compromise the discussion. Earlier in the chapter we talked about Simon, the head of geography who had to conduct a review of his friend and colleague Steve. By modelling the process with Simon, Louise, the deputy head, has illustrated the steps that Simon will have to follow to manage the performance of Steve. It will only be through regular discussion of the outcomes of meetings between Simon and Steve that Louise will be in a position to challenge and support the implementation of the performance management system. Meeting with people to discuss their performance should be an integral part of every manager's role (at whatever level). Those who are the subject of the meeting have to develop the professional maturity to respond to the issues presented.

_____ Conclusion _____

In this chapter we have talked about how to get going, what to talk about and how to keep records. Getting going is perhaps the easiest bit because it involves setting up meetings with people, telling them why, and holding a conversation. Keeping it all going is difficult because it is time intensive but a very necessary element of the job. Although it does demand a time commitment it will save time in the long term. The meetings that are set up are about performance management, but the discussions should lead on to debates on a whole range of issues, as the case studies have illustrated. By having a persistent and consistent dialogue then difficult things do not seem as hard to say or discuss. Department and team meetings are also smoother and more effective because there is regular dialogue about the things that matter. In addition, linking the performance review system to threshold standards means that for those progressing towards threshold application there is an alignment of the evidence to the application. For post-threshold staff, there is a basis for progress and review.

There is a temptation to make performance management all about accountability. As individuals we have an accountability for the work that we do in return for the remuneration we receive. As professionals we have an obligation to respond to feedback that helps us to do our jobs better and to take responsibility for the development of ourselves and that of others. This is performance management.

———— Reference ————

Handy, L., Devine, M. and Heath, L. (1996) *360 Degree Feedback: Unguided Missile or Powerful Weapon?*, Ashridge Management Research Group.

chapter eight

Linking staff development to performance management

Reflection and critical incidents

Feedback

Keeping a personal portfolio

Linking performance management to training and development

Conclusion

Getting people to reflect on incidents, enabling them to think about what has happened, allowing them to consider what has worked well and what needs to be improved, helping them move forward and progress – these are the hallmarks of effective performance management. If individuals are able to reflect on their work, then there can be much improved performance.

Reflection and critical incidents

This book has emphasised how the performance management process is an essential tool to bring about that reflection. Where individuals can be helped to develop their own internal review processes then the process is even more powerful. The model presented in Chapter 3 of how to move from a directing mode through tutoring, supporting and delegating provides the framework for the discussion. Going through a particular incident or an issue is sometimes a very painful exercise for a person but an opportunity that should not be missed.

To get people used to the idea of self-reflection and discussing their own performance, role play exercises can be very useful. Although not to everyone's taste, if carefully chosen they can bring about a discussion of the principles of coaching and indeed the way in which we develop others. They can be particularly useful with a group of staff brought together as part of an INSET session.

First, a group should discuss what staff development is. This is to dispel the notion that it is just about going on courses, and to get people used to the idea of learning through experience. A useful question here is 'What are the approved behaviours in your school and how do you know?' In one group a delegate said that missing deadlines was approved behaviour because it meant that an individual had more time to do the work, with no consequence. Although this was something of an indictment of his school's leadership, it provided a useful discussion into the way our actions convey our values and what this means for us as leaders. So by asking questions related to an individual's experience of school, we can gain information on what happened, what action was taken (or what did not happen) and how this affected the person's thinking. This should be followed up by asking people what action they expected, and why they think that this is the right thing to do, so providing a context for reflecting on critical incidents and developing the reflective process.

Second, ask people what their expectations are of others. Put simply, do they see the leadership role as being something that directly affects people's thinking and behaviour? The key here is to think about what happened to them and what their expectations are. One way to address this is to do some role play. People work in groups of three and each person plays a particular role. One person acts as the member of staff who is the subject, another as the person having the discussion and the third observes the discussion and makes notes. Then after the role plays have taken place the observations are shared and learning points extracted.

The following case studies can be used in role play exercises.

CASE STUDY 1

Max Wellbright

You are Max Wellbright. You are 28 and a confident high-flying maths teacher. You have achieved 80 per cent grades A*–C at GCSE this year and 70 per cent A–E at A level. You have helped three pupils go to Oxbridge to study maths. You graduated from Durham with a 2.1 and have always viewed yourself as a high achiever with ambition. Your reports have been glowing. In particular they praised your ability to teach, achieve high academic results and organise your workload. The deputy head says that you are the most organised teacher he has seen for 25 years. The only criticisms you have ever received are that you can sometimes be too blunt with parents about poor-performing, low-ability pupils. You also have a tendency to fly off the handle with colleagues when they have arrived late for meetings that you were chairing, or with whom you have disagreed, and you are sometimes too direct – thinking your opinion of how to run the school is best.

The post of head of year 11 has come up at the school and you have decided to apply. It is a TLR1 post remunerated at £11,000 which means you and your girlfriend will be able to buy a flat. The job does not entail too much extra work – just the odd discipline problem, some more reports for parents' evenings, etc. In addition, it would be your first rung on to the management ladder and to becoming a head.

The key competencies of the job are the abilities to:

- develop the academic and all-round skills of the pupils;
- develop the levels of self-esteem and the social skills of the pupils;
- work as a team member with the school management team;
- increase the number of pupils at the school;
- organise the pastoral effort for your year group.

Your mentor, the deputy head, has asked you for a meeting, presumably to give you some tips on how to handle the interview and develop into the job. How would you prepare?

There are a number of questions that are raised by this case study. First, Max expects to be told how to get the job – but is the deputy's role to tell him how to get the job or to tell him that he does not have the skills and experience to do so? The consequence of the former is that he will get a nasty surprise when he does not get the job (as presumably he won't) and feel resentment towards the deputy head who was not honest with him; or, if he gets the job, may have a very difficult time as he does not appear to be ready for such a role. If this is the first time that Max has received any feedback on his performance then it will be a shock and there may be some resentment as he may feel a little foolish. Does the deputy head see it as their role to facilitate Max getting the job or to advise him not to apply? Of course the 'correct' answer is to enable Max to reach his own conclusion, having been presented with a range of discussion points on which he can reflect. Getting Max to respond to some possible scenarios ('How would you respond if a parent said this . . .' and so on) is one way that Max can be guided through this meeting. However, if Max is used to discussing incidents and events with someone, then this potentially very difficult meeting will be less demanding (on both sides) and the leadership potential of this teacher can be harnessed.

The second case study is very different – a young teacher who is keen to progress but is someone who has a very different skill set.

CASE STUDY 2

Jemima Jollygood

Jemima Jollygood is 27 and is in her second year of teaching. She has a post-graduate degree in history from the University of Cardiff. She is a late entrant to the profession – she originally went to Birmingham University to study medicine but left after nine months on the course. You are her line manager.

Jemima really loves teaching history – she has a real passion for the subject and she is very insistent on the highest standards of academic rigour with pupils in her class. However, when you were talking to Colin Cranmer he said that the class she taught last year only seem to have studied Elizabeth 1 – and does not know anything about Mary, Queen of Scots.

Jemima spends a great deal of her time marking – you see her arrive in the morning with what looks like three sets of books every day. She works very hard indeed: you see her in the staffroom at briefing and the rest of the time she's in her classroom. Her classroom displays have always been really superb and she has been an excellent collaborator in the history department. When you leave for home at 6.00 p.m., or later sometimes, her car is still in the car park. This year she has taken on the job of being deputy head of year – there wasn't really much competition.

Last evening you went to ask her about a couple of things and were surprised that her classroom, normally very tidy and well organised, looked a complete state. She said that she wants to apply to be second in history when this job is advertised at the end of this term and asked if she can come to talk to you about how she's getting on.

The key competencies of this post are to:

- write schemes of work of key stage 3 history;
- monitor the work of key stage 3 history;
- work as a team member with the humanities management team;
- increase the number of students opting for history at key stage 4.

As her head of faculty, you are concerned about Jemima's work. How will you prepare for this meeting?

Again, there are a number of questions raised by this case study. We have a teacher who is working very hard indeed but there is the suggestion of a crisis – her normal habits have changed, and the outward sign is a messy classroom. By structuring a meeting with Jemima to discuss her workload and her approach, there is the opportunity to harness the energy and commitment she has. What is important for the head of faculty is to reflect on how this young teacher has reached this stage – how has her workload been managed and what might be done differently to ensure that she (and indeed others) has an appropriate work/life balance?

CASE STUDY 3

Wendy Miller

Wendy is the school receptionist. She has been working at the school for 12 years and is always punctual for work – never early, but never late. One of her tasks is to answer the telephone and take messages. People find her writing rather difficult to read and she can be abrupt with colleagues and with parents. One of the other reception staff has complained that Wendy never helps anyone else out – she expects other people to help her (for example, if the telephone rings and she is dealing with a visitor she expects others to answer the phone), but will never say thank you or acknowledge any other member of the administration team.

As office manager you have the task of meeting with Wendy to discuss a problem that has arisen. A parent has told the deputy head that Wendy said everyone was too busy to talk to her (the parent) – there's no record of the parent calling the school, but you did hear Wendy saying this to a parent.

As our school systems develop, the range of support staff and the role they play increase. Teachers used to managing other teachers will find themselves working alongside and managing support staff. It is important to remember that support staff have not had the same training as teachers; in addition, while a teacher's life is dominated by working with children, a member of the administration team may have little or infrequent contact with children. Teachers quickly have to become used to speaking with parents (if only for parents' evening) and the relationship with parents is an important dimension of the teacher–pupil–parent interface. Parents are often, quite rightly, very concerned at anything that affects their child – this case study is a useful focus for discussion because it examines that sensitive relationship between parents and the school.

The case study also raises the issue of how to tackle an incident where a complaint has been made about a person on the basis of a report – there is even more potential for conflict here because the incident is about interpersonal relations. Tackling people about instances where things have gone wrong can make people defensive, while for those who have to investigate it can cause apprehension. However, people do expect their line managers to take things up with them – and certainly parents expect action to be taken when things go wrong.

The way forward with such an incident is to ask the person to comment on what has been said – to ask them to reflect on how the person who has made the complaint has been made to feel. It is important not to be drawn into a discussion about why nothing has been said before – this kind of debate can be useful but will often be a distraction from the core issue.

These three case studies illustrate how people can be given the opportunity to think about issues. In role play, one person will be member of staff who is at the centre, another the person discussing it with them, and the third will observe the interaction between the two parties. Encouraging people to think about the circumstances that led up to the discussion, what they achieved by having the discussion and how they would change their practice in future is the paradigm for self-reflection.

Feedback

The model of performance management in this book is one where we take every opportunity to discuss strategy, implementation and practice with colleagues, so the principle of reflection is one that becomes a natural activity. Giving people feedback is an important part of the process. Starr (2003) talks about the pejorative use of the word 'feedback' – if we say 'I'd like to give you some feedback' then this is often a prelude to a negative conversation. Starr suggests how giving critical remarks can be phrased in different ways. For example:

- 'You keep upsetting people because you're so blunt with your remarks.'
- 'When you told Mark he'd no chance of getting the job, I thought he appeared upset.'
- 'When you told Mark he'd no chance of getting the job, how do you think he felt?'

Most of us will wince at the thought of the first remark, while we can appreciate how the last way of phrasing the feedback would encourage some element of reflection.

We can take this as a model for three different ways of discussing an issue:

- What 'you' do and the effect 'you' have on others. This is highly subjective and might be greeted with hostility and denial (the person could deny that they are blunt, or comment that they are simply a 'straight talker' or 'call a spade a spade').
- What 'you' do and what 'I' think of the effect. This is a better way to engage with the person, but it introduces another opinion. A response to this might be 'Well, I didn't think he appeared upset' and the discussion will become about what one person thinks has happened rather than about the particular incident or issue.

- What 'you' do and what do 'you' think is the effect. This gives the opportunity to explore the impact of one person's behaviour on another. It is an approach where an individual is encouraged to think about the effect that their action has on a person, rather than starting off with an assertion that their actions have had an effect. You may move to saying something like 'I thought he appeared upset', but this will emerge from discussion rather than being an assertion that can be disputed.

This is reflective practice: looking at what we do and considering the effect that we have on others, but also thinking about it before we do it and using the process to reflect on incidents that have passed.

Keeping a personal portfolio

To some people, the idea of keeping a personal portfolio is very natural and obvious. One of our colleagues keeps a file – complete with plastic wallets – where every performance-related document is catalogued (including thank-you notes and cards from colleagues and parents). Going through this file it is possible to see how this person's career and professional development – one outcome from this was that she found it very straightforward to present evidence for threshold assessment because it was already ordered.

Teachers joining the profession over recent years have had career entry profiles that have enabled them to take the learning from their initial training through to their induction year. Throughout the induction year there are formal reports and it is good practice for newly qualified teachers to compile these into a formal record. We have suggested that performance management reviews are carried out under the headings for threshold assessment; again, if these are held together then they form a coherent record of their work.

Linking performance management to training and development

Performance review is an important process because it facilitates a discussion on progress made over a year. It is essential both as an individual's right but also for pay purposes. One outcome from a performance review is the need for further training and development. Of course, inviting people to say what courses they might like to go on can be a very risky business because it will create a very expensive and scattergun approach to staff development. In addition, when teachers go on courses during the school day then their classes have to be covered; for members of the support staff, essential duties may be covered but generally people will return to a desk with yesterday's work as well as the normal amount for the day. So there has to be a balance between professional development and the needs of the organisation, including the demands of classes that have a right to be taught.

Deciding who has the opportunity to go on what course is a difficult task to complete alone. It is therefore advisable to have some form of prioritisation process that can determine how the limited INSET budget will be spent. The principles of INSET, in order, are that:

- It should address elements of the school improvement plan. One way to achieve this is to have a system where applications for INSET are referenced to the school improvement plan. Making some kind of tenuous reference to a plan is easy, but it is more difficult to discriminate those activities that will really enable the plan to be implemented. Some of the training needs are obvious – for example, examination board updating sessions are useful because they provide a useful reference point for feedback in public examinations. Where a school improvement plan has specific development (for example, it might be to develop Assessment for Learning) then by identifying a course or conference and selecting a member of staff who can lead on such development is a way of linking the plan with training and development.

- It should improve the pupil experience. Again, making some kind of tenuous reference to pupil experience is easy, but the impact of a development opportunity needs to be judged in terms of how many pupils will benefit from an improvement and how it relates to school priorities. Since there should be an explicit link between improving the pupil experience and the school improvement plan, prioritising development that improves both is ideal.

- It should address individual staff professional needs. Teaching is a profession that relies on professional development having been carried out by others. Frequently, teachers have to move schools to gain a promotion – it is likely that people on the leadership team will have worked in three or more schools. Indeed, having worked at more than one school is often a criterion for selection. We rely, therefore, on other people developing staff so that at our own schools we can select them to do the roles we need to undertake. Without this altruistic approach to staff development, the heads of department, heads of year, leadership team and headteachers simply would not be there. Within our own schools, we need to decide which courses to prioritise. There are some that are more obvious than others: NPQH (National Professional Qualification for Headteachers), LfM (Leading from the Middle) and the Developing Leaders Programme (Specialist Schools and Academies Trust) are three that have a hard currency in the INSET and professional development world. So do courses leading to certificates, diplomas and higher degrees. There is also a range of training courses that fit squarely into the procedural category, such as timetabling and information management courses. Without these there is no succession planning and therefore these need to be woven into the training and development arrangements. Of course, individuals will have specific needs as well – people will often benefit from going on behaviour management courses or on refresher courses.

■ There should be an accountability for the money that is spent. A relatively straightforward methodology is to compile a spreadsheet where each development activity is linked to the school improvement plan. Then it becomes possible to see how much money from the INSET budget has been spent to support each element of the plan. There is also the greater accountability to the organisation, so whenever a person engages in development activity there should be opportunities to share or 'cascade' the knowledge to other staff. Some schools have formal evaluation activities and create opportunities for people to share the information, but in practice this is difficult because of the lack of time for training and development.

Training and development can be a challenge because there are many demands on a limited budget. Add to this the somewhat sporadic nature of training and development opportunities that arise (the post seems to deliver a fresh set of course flyers daily!) and the task of creating a coherent plan is complicated further. One of the best opportunities for staff development – and for most schools the biggest INSET budget sector – is the five-day allocation for staff training purposes. A crude analysis of the staffing budget will quickly show how much an INSET day represents in terms of money to be spent. We have calculated that the five INSET days cost about £9000–£10,000 per day in staff costs (divide the staffing bill by 195); for a staff of 55 it represents a total of 275 days (or the equivalent to employing a teacher for about four terms!). For a primary school with a teaching staff of, say, 10 people, it represents 50 days work. Taken over a year this is a considerable sum of money.

Joyce et al. (1999) referred to five major components to training (reviewed by Joyce and Showers). These five components are a way of planning out a series of staff development activities.

- *Presentation of theory.* By presenting the theory we provide people with the rationale – a conceptual framework and basis of an approach to teaching and learning. This does not necessarily have to be in the form of a lecture or a presentation where someone is brought in from 'outside' (i.e. a guest speaker) to expound a particular theory. Although it can be very useful to invite a guest speaker to come and talk to the staff about a particular development or way of thinking, it is even more powerful if the expertise exists in the school. If people hear a colleague talk and share their knowledge it creates the idea of the school as a learning community. The idea of a 'theory' can also be taken more broadly, perhaps restating the aims and values of the school, or a session on the school improvement plan, placed in the context of organisational theory or development. This first session raises awareness but provides the context for the next stage.

- *Modelling and demonstrations.* The next stage is the enactment of a new teaching skill or strategy. This approach can be broadened to incorporate presentations where individuals and groups talk about what they have done – explaining how they have approached a particular issue, what has happened and what progress has been made. This is important because it shows that the theory is a contextual framework that underpins practice, but also that the practice underpins theory because it works in the classroom. It is vital because it is about sharing ideas; Fullan (2004) talks about this as a system knowledge and system identity. System knowledge is what we know about the way in which our school (i.e. the systems, the classrooms, the students, the teachers, the support staff) works, while system identity is where we see ourselves as part of the improvement process because we understand how it works and what our part is in bringing about improvement. Thus Fullan says: 'when best ideas are freely available and cultivated, and when collective identity prospers, we have a change in the very context of the local system . . . And system change is the kind of change that keeps on giving.' There is quite a leap from performance management to the kind of sharing that Fullan espouses, but by planning out learning experiences for staff who are being taught by their peers, we create and sustain the learning community that is networked across the school.

- *Practice in the workshop or under simulated conditions.* The next stage is to provide some simulated conditions for the practice to be developed. Role play is an example of providing a simulated condition. By setting groups of teachers and other school staff particular tasks and discussion questions then some of the processes of practice can be developed through this medium. However, there is no question that if the benefits of whole-school INSET are going to be realised, then there has to be an imperative to move on to the next stage. The school improvement plan is the principal vehicle for doing this but there needs to be some 'next step'. In the assessment for learning programme the first step is to talk about what assessment for learning is, and then ask people who have been trying out some of the ideas to talk about what they have been doing. The next stage is to ask groups of teachers to decide on an assessment for learning focus and to plan it out. People then write a brief summary of what they are going to do. This forms the basis of the future development because then we can go back to people to ask them about how it is going.

- *Structured feedback.* Whenever we plan any staff development we need to plan in how we are going to give people feedback on how it is going. The performance management system we have described throughout this book is just that. The principles of discussion, reflection and feedback are very important if the theory that is presented is going to move from something that someone else does (i.e. the best practice that represents what others do) to behaviour and practice that embody what everyone does. Having structured feedback programmed into the development activity means that a 'practice–feedback–practice' sequence can be developed.

- *Coaching for classroom application.* When we think of our schools do we think of them as being about pupils or for pupils? Do we see the work that goes on as being progressive (in that it moves forward and is transforming) or regressive (in that it perpetuates a status quo where everything stays the same and the systems are designed to keep everything normal)? If staff development does not impact on what happens in the classroom then it is pointless, and if the process of staff development does not incorporate the principles of coaching for classroom application it is redundant activity. When designing development programmes we must think about how people will translate and transfer their knowledge and practice to the classroom situation. More broadly we have to consider the capacity and capability of individuals and groups to bring this about. As Fullan and Hargreaves (1992) wrote: 'Teachers ... are more than mere bundles of knowledge, skill and technique ... Teachers are people too.' If, for example, the ideas of assessment for learning are going to form part of the rubric of classroom experience then those who are new to the practice need guidance on what to do, how to do it and the encouragement and support to use the new skills. Coaching can be provided by a range of people (in the case of assessment for learning, then teaching assistants are very well placed to do this), helping people to analyse the way to teach, the approach to be taken and the very specific plans to help the students adapt to the new approach.

We advocate a structured approach to staff INSET not only because it represents a tremendous opportunity for the whole staff group to work together but also because with no plan there is the risk of wasting a huge amount of money. By making the link between the school improvement plan and the INSET activity explicit we can create Caldwell's (2005) 'domains of practice' – where different areas of the school's work are developed simultaneously and reinforced through theory, modelling, exemplification and practice: we create an organisation that builds its own expertise. Of course the school has to guard against becoming introverted and introspective. Working with partners in education, for example the Specialist Schools Trust or National College for School Leaders, is an effective way to ensure that policy is formulated by taking the best from the national debate but customising it to suit the local context.

Conclusion

What we have described is a way of planning out staff development to bring about organisational goals. By creating a framework of coaching and individualised development we create a parallel structure to the way we work with students. Personalising learning with students is about making sure that 'every aspect of teaching and support is designed around a pupil's needs' (Miliband, in Hargreaves, 2005) and this is nothing less than the path to the transformation of the secondary system. We can be optimistic about achieving the objectives of INSET if we base our planning on theory, practice and coaching. By linking the three together, using the performance management system to reinforce and support staff development, we provide a process where knowledge and learning are embedded in the practice of our school.

———— References ————

Caldwell, B. (2005) *New Enterprise Logic of Schools*, iNet, Specialist Schools Trust, London.

Fullan, M. (2004) *Systems Thinkers in Action: Moving Beyond the Standards Plateau*, DfES, London (www.standards.dfes.gov.uk/innovation-unit).

Fullan, M. and Hargreaves, A. (1992) *What's Worth Fighting For in Your School?* Open University Press, Buckingham.

Hargreaves, D. (2005) *Personalising Learning: 3. Learning to Learn and the New Technologies* iNet, Specialist Schools Trust, London.

Joyce, B., Calhoun, E. and Hopkins, D. (1999) *The New Structure of School Improvement: Inquiring Schools and Achieving Students*, Open University Press, Buckingham.

Starr, J. (2003) *The Coaching Manual*, Prentice Hall, Harlow.

chapter nine

The future of performance management

Leadership programmes

Competencies and behaviours

Teamwork

Conclusion

159

In the preceding pages we have considered how we have arrived at the national policy for performance management for teachers that we have now; how we might go about creating a policy; a framework for carrying out the performance management discussions that are the essential component of the whole process; how we might frame job descriptions that can usefully form the core of the process; the specific considerations for headteacher and support staff performance management; and assessment and self-assessment. Our intention has been to help the reader to reflect upon their own policy and procedures rather than prescribe how it should be done. In this final chapter we will consider some of the pitfalls that may conspire to undermine the best laid plans for a thoughtful and effective approach to performance management.

There are a number of possible risks to the process:

- *Inertia*. It requires a significant amount of effort to manage the performance of a team member. There are meetings to be scheduled and prepared for, and if it is a teacher who is being managed then there are lesson observations to be carried out and fed back. All these elements need to be written up, and the writing up is done in the knowledge that the team member is going to be very sensitive about what is written. Given all these factors, it is scarcely surprising that some team leaders find many other priorities for their attention before performance management. However, beware the team leaders who say that they 'don't have time': performance management should be a priority activity for team leaders, and team leaders will always find time for their priorities.

- *Critical feedback*. The things that we find most difficult are those that bring us into conflict with others. Providing critical feedback inevitably places us in conflict with those we manage. Perhaps the simplest thing for most of us is therefore simply to avoid giving that feedback. If you are the headteacher then you must make sure you read the performance review statements as they come in, and watch out for where issues have not been tackled – these statements should be returned. All team leaders need to be trained in giving feedback and dealing with conflict. They need to understand that this is part of the job and that their team members expect it of them.

- *Objective setting*. Objectives should be central to the team members work and should define the critical outcomes for their work over the review period. They are not additional items, they are not simply a list of training courses the team member wishes to attend, and, above all, they are not actions for other people – what the team member thinks will make their job easier!

It would be very easy for the whole performance management process to relapse into the appraisal process that preceded it. There is also an incorrect emphasis in the teacher association literature on professional development. This is not what performance management is about – it is about managing the performance of the staff within the school. Improvements in performance are likely to come about through training and development opportunities, and so this will form part of the process, but we do need to be clear that performance management is about achieving the goals of the school through those who work within it.

This book is about the total performance management process, but in the final pages we want to discuss what we can learn from other organisations, and also examine the link between leadership development and performance management. Tranter (2003) explains the link between performance management and leadership programmes, using research undertaken with the National College for School Leadership (NCSL). The awareness that leadership of our schools is subject to huge challenges, and that there is a paucity of applicants for some of the more challenging posts, together with a realisation that headship has had radical changes in recent years, have all led to a rethink about how the profession prepares people for leadership. The core purpose of headship is to provide professional leadership for a school, so securing the school's success and improvement, and ensuring high-quality education for all its pupils and improved standards of learning and achievement. The enormity of the task, which includes unlocking the potential from the nation's children, is considerable; if schools are to equip society with the next generation ready for the future then new ways have to be found to lead and to manage.

Leadership programmes

The Fast Track teaching programme is an established part of the government's strategy to identify and promote people in the profession. The principle is that it will identify and reward existing teachers with ambition and potential. It focuses on the rapid development of professional excellence in the classroom, as well as school leadership. The careers of teachers on the Fast Track programme are centrally managed. The idea is that teachers will have access to specific mentoring and support and connection to a national network of teachers across the Fast Track programme. Teachers on the Fast Track programme agree not to be bound by the same restrictions on working hours that apply to other teachers.

The Fast Track programme has two main elements. First, the central support team formulates and delivers a wide range of professional development opportunities. Second, the team also runs the overall management and implementation of the programme, monitoring and evaluating the services provided. The aim is to recruit the most talented teachers, with the intention that approximately 5 per cent of the teaching workforce in the future will have been developed via this route. Assessment is against a standard of performance measured by Fast Track competencies. The Fast Track competencies and values are as follows:

- Analysis and problem solving: identifies solutions to problems and takes responsibilities for making decisions.

- Conceptual thinking: thinks beyond the immediate solution and identifies new and improved ways of doing things.

- Ensuring the delivery of quality results: sets high standards for themselves and others and ensures that they are achieved.

- Communicating effectively: communicates effectively both orally and in writing, capturing the interest and enthusiasm of different audiences.

- Influencing others: is able to persuade and influence other people.

- Developing and enabling others: continually encourages others to perform at the best of their abilities and challenges underperformance.

- Team working and building relationships: builds and contributes to highly effective working relationships with individuals, within and across teams.

- Confidence and resilience: demonstrates self-confidence in their ability to succeed, maintaining energy and enthusiasm in highly challenging situations.

- Commitment to self-development: shows a commitment to their own learning and takes responsibility for their own professional development.

Talent-spotting people with top leadership potential takes place in many employment areas. For example, leading multinational company SDR has a Top Talent programme. This programme operates for people who have been in post for a minimum of two years and is only open to those with first-class degrees and A-level scores of 28 points or more (under the old method of scoring, this organisation still uses grade A = 10 points, grade B = 8 points and so on). People have to be nominated by their superiors and have a consistently high level of performance throughout their time with the company. Although open to anyone with this two-year minimum service, the programme has only recruited people with more than five but less than ten years' experience in the company.

The assessment process goes through a defined sequence, beginning with psychometric testing. This includes a number of tests. First, the 16PF (Cattell) is administered by a psychologist. The applicant undergoes an interview based on the outcomes of this test. Typically the interview lasts for two to three hours and focuses on the individual's values and principles. This is to assess the applicant against three core competencies – drive, values and principles. Second, the applicant takes a critical reasoning test. This is typically the Watson-Glaser Critical Thinking Appraisal Test. This is designed to test a person's maximum rather than a typical performance (i.e. what the ceiling of their ability is). The questions in these tests include the extraction of data from complex numerical and verbal material. The core competencies tested are inference, recognition of assumptions, deduction, interpretation and evaluation of arguments. Other tests include numerical reasoning. The outcome of all these tests is an ability and aptitude profile. (For a fuller discussion see Edenborough, 1999.)

The final element in this assessment is a criteria-based interview. The candidate has to select an event (a project or a significant incident) and evaluate it. At least two people interview the applicant about this event. The interview takes about three hours and explores the leadership issues, the management choices and the implications of these decisions. The assessment is an analysis of all of these elements.

Applicants are then plotted on axes – potential (horizontal) and talent (vertical). For those in the upper quadrant (high talent and high potential), their progress is closely monitored and regular reports are compiled. Where opportunities for projects arise then people on this high talent list are automatically considered. The emphasis is on developing people with leadership skills that can be transferred across any part of the corporate empire. Appraisal is six-monthly (with monthly reporting sessions) and the appraisal statements follow the individual from one sector of the company to another. People who do not meet the exacting profile are given feedback on their performance in the assessment and can reapply for assessment after one year.

The scheme is still in its infancy; successful candidates are very well remunerated and enjoy a high level of development input but those who do not meet the criteria frequently feel that their careers will be limited under this scheme.

The strength of the Fast Track system is that it seeks to identify those people who have the necessary skills and attributes to be the school leaders of the future. It uses a range of assessment techniques, based on a set of defined characteristics that are judged important. The question is whether such people can be truly effective if their expectation is to be in post for a short time – indeed, whether it is possible to have any kind of long-lasting effectiveness in such a short time at all. In contrast, the corporate programme has the advantage of selecting people for the Top Talent programme when they have been with the company for a period (it is open to those who have been in the company for two years but successful applicants typically have worked for five to ten years). A key difference between work in schools and that of other businesses (public or private sector) is that all the planning for those outside the leadership team takes place alongside what is already a big job of being a teacher. In other spheres it is less common for people who are leaders to have this dual role. The corporate programmes also start from the principle that talent is spotted from those already in post and known to be good at their present job, assuming that the people who are very good at their job are those with the potential to lead others. The Fast Track scheme on the other hand places a huge emphasis on those with the potential to be very good at their job. Company schemes can also cause difficulties for those who are unsuccessful in their application to the programme. These people can feel that they are 'finished' as far as the company is concerned; the Fast Track system avoids this by being separate from the schools that employ the teachers.

As SDR is a major player in the multinational corporate world then people's careers can be planned strategically. Opportunities can be found to give people the development they need by sending them for a short or long period to work in a particular division. The nature of multinational commercial activity is that problems are usually of a short-term nature. There are long-term strategic decisions to be taken and addressed (such as market change, product development, technological impact, and so on) but broadly the problems that need to be fixed fall within the scope of the company's own remit. Rarely are problems in education this straightforward. The cycle of the school year means that the process of planning, monitoring, evolution and review is one that has at least a 12-month duration.

Teachers' careers also depend hugely on the opportunities that arise; we do not have a system where teachers are 'posted' to schools. In contrast, in Singapore heads of department are nominated by the principal for consideration to be a vice-principal. The Ministry of Education receives such nominations and considers the nomination and all the information that it has on the teacher (this includes their performance reviews, results of their teaching and academic qualifications). If appointed as a vice-principal, then the teacher can be posted to any school in Singapore. After two years there is a formal review; if the person has made good progress then they can be nominated for training to be a principal. If the performance is less than satisfactory then they are given a further period of two years or can be returned to being a head of department. If accepted on the principal programme, the person will take a nine-month full-time training course on leadership and management in schools. Then the person is posted to a school as principal. Again, the person can be posted to any school in Singapore. Their performance is monitored by the cluster superintendent and if unsatisfactory the person returns to being a head of department. The maximum tenure at any school for a principal is six years, and principals can be moved to any school at any time. Principals and vice-principals do not teach. In England, schools decide for themselves who they employ and therefore a teacher's career has this interdependency with the system within which it operates.

Competencies and behaviours

What the company scheme outlined above and the Fast Track scheme have in common is an emphasis on skills attributes and competencies for the leadership of the company or organisation. This emphasis on competencies is an approach that is being developed in a number of organisations as they seek to address the issues of recruitment, selection, retention and career progression. One organisation is the civil service, which like SDR has sufficient scope to develop schemes across the whole of the service but, like schools, has a longer time frame in which to solve its problems (and some of these problems, as in schools, are located only partially within its own locus of control).

Trying to get the best from people is one of the real management challenges. One approach has been the competency model: the principle is that we can identify the jobs, the tasks, the attributes that are required for a role and then assess people against the model and use the model to plan their development. The core competencies approach calls on companies or organisations to identify the distinctive and differentiating competencies that lie at the heart of their operation. However, identifying an organisation's core competencies is fraught with difficulties. Part of the difficulty lies in the distinction between personal competencies and corporate competencies. Often it is easiest to start with the personal, because these are relatively straightforward to establish. Then an organisation can synthesise the skills of its employees into the generic competencies that apply to the organisation as a whole. Crainer and Dearlove (2001) argue that a weakness to the core competency model is that an organisation's critical competencies and insights often reside in a small number of people, who are not necessarily senior managers. In a knowledge-intensive and information-intensive age, this is increasingly the case. The danger is that if the people depart, so too do the competencies.

Competencies are not the only way in which the work of teachers and school leaders has been referenced. In 1998 the Teacher Training Agency (TTA) published a set of National Standards for headteachers, subject leaders, special educational needs coordinators (SENCO) and qualified teacher status (QTS). These have since been used widely to determine training programmes, for compiling job descriptions, and as models for appraisal. The purpose of all four sets of standards was set down by the then chief executive of the TTA, Anthea Millett, and was designed to help teachers and headteachers to identify and focus in-service training needs and set targets for improvement, as well as provide a basis for the recognition of expertise and a means of setting expectations for future professional development.

In 2001 Hay McBer published *Models of Excellence for School Leaders*. The behaviours in the Hay McBer framework relate to all roles in the same way, so behaviours should be evident at all levels. Although it is difficult to compare school leader competencies with specific-outcome headteacher standards, an analysis of the National Standards and the Hay McBer model – presented below – does highlight pervasive themes:

- The strength of the National Standards model is in some ways its conciseness, emphasising that the core purpose is to secure improvement and success. The Hay McBer model acknowledges the leadership dimension in that it emphasises the need for effective teams and visionary leadership qualities. The National Standards emphasis is on outcomes that can be assessed quantitatively, whereas the Hay McBer model requires a more discursive and reflective analysis. Alimo-Metcalfe and Alban-Metcalfe (2000) write that transformational leadership has been found to have a significantly greater impact on individuals' motivation, satisfaction, commitment and performance than 'transactional leadership'. But where they are combined then they become the basis for many effective development programmes. They argue that one of the major reasons why transformational leadership research has been undertaken was a concern about the preoccupation in organisations with management competencies. While these are essential for management effectiveness, they focus primarily on *transactional* (their emphasis) leadership components. What is needed is the identification of additional leadership dimensions that inform managerial development and the design of selection, and performance management processes.

- The emphasis in the National Standards model is on what constitutes effective provision. Implicit in the Hay McBer model is the view that understanding is the key attribute.

———— Teamwork ————

An important element in job descriptions is the interface between one role and another. To analyse this we need a definition of teamwork that will be sustainable. It means thinking about the relationship in new ways. West and Allen (1997) introduced the concept of a 'work team' that is characterised as follows:

- Team members have shared objectives in relation to their work.
- Team members interact with each other in order to achieve those shared objectives.
- Team members have more or less well-defined roles, some of which are differentiated from one another.
- Teams have organisational identity – that is, they have a defined organisational function and see themselves as a group within a larger organisation.
- Teams are not so large that they would be better defined as an organisation.

The role of the team leader is crucial here. It is about ensuring that there is sufficient clarity on the nature of the role and the function of the team. Before selecting personnel for a particular team, attention needs to be given to the design or structure of the work that the team members will do and the roles they will occupy. Typically, teachers are recruited and selected to work as part of a group because they appear to have the particular set of technical skills and experience deemed necessary for particular aspects of the job. This is, of course, entirely reasonable. Also reasonable, however, would be an examination of the degree to which candidates have the personal characteristics necessary to work effectively as part of the team.

All those working in schools are constantly engaged in change; there is no steady state. The continual drive to raise standards, the perpetual debate on how things can be done better, the imperative to add value, means that, to an extent, all managers are 'turnaround managers'. By considering the expectations and the task focus of the team as a whole, the leadership model becomes clearer.

Conclusion

The process of performance management is an entitlement for those who work within the school. If they are teachers, then there is the somewhat sharper matter of a statutory link to the performance-related pay element of the upper pay spine – members of the leadership team and those on the upper pay spine cannot progress up their pay spine without a performance review against previously set objectives. But even without that edge, all members of staff should expect the opportunity to talk one to one with their line manager on a regular basis, and they have the right to expect feedback on the standard of their work. It is therefore incumbent upon all team leaders to take this responsibility seriously, and it is consequently incumbent upon the school leadership to ensure the process is suitably monitored and that the whole thing is made to happen.

At the end of the cycle the team member should expect to have a formal statement of their team leader's view of their progress through the year, along with a set of objectives. There may also be recommendations about development and training opportunities the team member should have to help them achieve the objectives. That the statement and objectives are agreed is desirable, but there is no requirement – the document is written as the judgement of the team leader and the set of objectives is set by the team leader.

The Five Year Strategy for Children and Learners (July 2004, ref. CM6272) set down five promises that the Government was making for the future. These are:

■ Personalised learning for everyone: 'Every student should, within their school, have excellent teaching that suits them, building on what they know, fitting them for what they aspire to and helping them reach their full potential', the report reads.

- Greater choice of schools: The aim is to have decent schools wherever people live; more new schools; an independent specialist schools system; and 200 independently managed academies to replace inadequate secondary schools.

- More places in popular schools: Successful schools can opt to expand and there will be a fast-track system in place for expansion.

- Greater subject choice between 14 and 19, a richer curriculum and links beyond the classroom, including more high-quality vocational qualifications.

- Change to how schools teach: Strategies such as workforce reform and more structured professional development aim to improve secondary teaching still further.

The latter gives an indication as to the changes in the performance review system that is envisaged in the future; and for which the framework we have set down will prepare schools to accommodate. The Strategy argues that better teaching will come from investing in the workforce; fundamental to this improvement is excellent professional development for all teachers with an increasing emphasis on classroom observation, practice, training, coaching and mentoring. Teacher appraisal is likely to be renamed 'Teaching and Learning Review' (rather confusingly this might be abbreviated to TLR!). The principles are currently under development but are likely to be focused on improving classroom practice, providing teachers with the opportunities to mentor and coach other teachers. The link between development and progression will be explicit in future legislation and therefore the paradigm that we have argued as essential for effective performance management as part of a school improvement strategy is entirely concordant.

If we are to avoid performance management becoming a bureaucratic exercise then it is crucial that these principles are kept alive in the school. Only then will we see leaders and managers becoming increasingly confident in asserting their right to lead and manage and will we see the increasing professionalism of the workforce in schools. It is our contention that as a consequence of effective performance management then we will see rapid improvement in schools. The difficulty is how to ensure this happens. Monitoring performance management processes nationally has been the remit of the governors' external adviser on head-teacher performance management. It is unclear the extent to which this remit has been carried out effectively – certainly we have experienced no evidence of this element of the process. Performance management is a hidden dimension within the school; again, in our experience, it rarely features as part of good practice discussions between schools. It is taken as a given. How do we know that the principles of effective performance management are being adhered to – or indeed that they are not being adhered to? There needs to be a fuller sharing of systems and procedures between schools and it needs to be recognised more widely that this is the way to rapid school improvement. Under the New Relationship with Schools, the school improvement partner now has the responsibility for monitoring performance management systems. This is an excellent opportunity to push the matter up the agenda and provides an impetus to system-wide improvement. The prize is there for the taking – we must ensure we seize the moment.

_____ References and further reading _____

Alimo-Metcalfe, B. and Alban-Metcalfe, R. (2000) 'A new approach to assessing transformational leadership', *Selection Development Review*, vol. 16, no. 5 British Psychological Society.

Born, M. and Jansen, P. (1997) 'Selection and assessment during oganisational turnaround' in Herriot, P. and Anderson, N. *International Handbook of Selection and Assessment*, John Wiley, Chichester.

Crainer, S. and Dearlove, D. (2001) *Financial Times Handbook of Management*, Pearson Education, Harlow.

Edenborough, R. (1999) *Using Psychometrics: A Practical Guide to Testing and Assessment*, 2nd edition, Kogan Page, London.

Handy, C. (1995) *The Age of Unreason*, Arrow, London.

Hargreaves, D. (1972) *Interpersonal Relations and Education*, Routledge & Kegan Paul, London.

Hay McBer (2001) *Models of Excellence for School Leaders*, Hay Group, London.

Lodge, D. (1988) *Nice Work*, Penguin, London.

MacGilchrist, B., Myers, K. and Reed, J. (1997) *The Intelligent School*, Paul Chapman Publishing, London.

Noble, T. and Pym, B. (1970) 'Collegial authority and the receding locus of power' in Bush, T. (ed.) *Managing Education: Theory and Practice*, Open University Press, Buckingham.

Tranter, S. (2000) *From Teacher to Middle Manager*, Pearson Education, Harlow.

Tranter, S. (2003) *Talent Spotting: Recognising and Developing Leadership Potential*, NCSL, Nottingham.

Weber, M. (1947) 'Legal authority in a bureaucracy' in Bush, T. (ed.) *Managing Education: Theory and Practice*, Open University Press, Buckingham.

West, M. and Allen, N. (1997) 'Selecting for teamwork' in Herriot, P. and Anderson, N. *International Handbook of Selection and Assessment*, John Wiley, Chichester.

Sample job descriptions

Director of staff development

Head of subject

Year leader

Classroom teacher

Curriculum administrator

Director of staff development

Accountable to: deputy head (quality of teaching) and ultimately the headteacher.

The director of staff development is responsible for all aspects of staff development for all staff who have day-to-day classroom responsibility for students.

Core purpose

The core purpose of the director of staff development is to provide professional leadership and management for staff development to secure high-quality teaching, effective use of resources and improved standards of learning and achievement for all pupils.

Specific tasks

The specific tasks associated with the role of director of staff development are:

- induction of all new staff;
- leading and managing the induction programme of newly qualified teachers;
- leading and managing staff employed as part of the Graduate Recruitment Teacher (GRT) programme (the postholder will be responsible for the programme in school, working with the subject leader);
- leading and managing overseas trained teachers to successful Qualified Teacher Status (QTS) (the postholder will be responsible for the programme in school, working with the subject leader);
- leading and managing the continuing professional development of staff;
- leading the development and implementation of the teaching and learning policy for the school;
- leading and developing the teaching and learning development plan;
- managing the INSET budget.

Leading, managing and developing staff development
The tasks associated with the role of director of staff development are specifically to:

- lead the development and implementation of policies and practices in line with school policies;
- advise the headteacher and deputy headteacher of developments in teaching and learning;
- liaise with the deputy head (quality of learning) to plan, develop and ensure the effective delivery of ICT as a staff development task;
- prepare development plans as necessary;
- promote staff development in school and beyond;
- participate, where appropriate, in the XXX partnership programme;
- produce reports for the headteacher and deputy headteacher, as required.

The outcomes that are associated with this element are to lead staff development so that teachers will:

- be consistent in their practice;
- be consistent in their implementation of policies;
- use the outcomes of self-evaluation to develop practice that results in pupil progress;
- collaborate to implement development plans;
- be punctual to class;
- start the lesson with a register;
- set and assess work according to the school policies;
- have, where appropriate, a seating plan for all classes;
- behave, dress and represent the highest standards of professional conduct at all times;
- teach clearly structured lessons or sequences of work that interest and motivate pupils and which:

  - make learning objectives clear to pupils
  - employ interactive teaching methods and collaborative group work
  - promote active and independent learning that enables pupils to think for themselves, and to plan and manage their own learning;

- differentiate their teaching to meet the needs of pupils, including the more able and those with special educational needs (they may have guidance from an experienced teacher where appropriate);

- be able to support those who are learning English as an additional language, with the help of an experienced teacher where appropriate;

- take account of the varying interests, experiences and achievements of boys and girls, and pupils from different cultural and ethnic groups, to help pupils make good progress;

- organise and manage teaching and learning time effectively;

- organise and manage the physical teaching space, tools, materials, texts and other resources safely and effectively, with the help of support staff where appropriate;

- set high expectations for pupils' behaviour and establish a clear framework for classroom discipline to anticipate and manage pupils' behaviour constructively, and promote self-control and independence;

- use ICT effectively in their teaching;

- take responsibility for teaching a class or classes over a sustained and substantial period of time, teaching across the age and ability range for which they are trained;

- provide homework and other out-of-class work that consolidates and extends work carried out in the class and encourages pupils to learn independently;

- work collaboratively with specialist teachers and other colleagues and, with the help of an experienced teacher as appropriate, manage the work of teaching assistants or other adults to enhance pupils' learning;

- recognise and respond effectively to equal opportunities issues as they arise in the classroom, including by challenging stereotyped views, and by challenging bullying or harassment, following relevant policies and procedures.

The outcomes that are associated with this element are to lead staff development so that pupils will:

- actively participate in learning;

- produce work and assignments in response to curriculum demands (including homework);

- conform to the school's behaviour policy.

The outcomes that are associated with this element are to work as part of a team of heads of subject who:

- are consistent in their practice;
- share good practice with other subject leaders;
- act as role models in teaching pupils effectively;
- act as role models in managing pupils effectively;
- act as role models in demonstrating professional curriculum leadership.

Impact on educational progress of pupils beyond those
assigned to the teacher

The outcomes that are associated with this element are to lead staff development so that pupils will:

- achieve high standards in public examinations;
- progress to the next stage of their education with confidence and enthusiasm;
- show sustained improvement in the relevant subject;
- understand how to improve their studies;
- know their academic targets;
- be enthusiastic about the subject;
- contribute to the maintenance of a purposeful working environment.

Leading, developing and enhancing the teaching practice of
others and managing staff

The tasks associated with the role of director of staff development are specifically to:

- implement school policy on monitoring and evaluating staff development and the quality of teaching and learning – this will include undertaking lesson observation, giving feedback to staff and, where appropriate, setting targets to improve the quality of teaching;
- lead the production and updating of staff development programmes – these should ensure appropriate coverage, continuity and progression so that the needs of individuals and groups are managed, including those on Fast Track and those requiring additional support;
- coordinate the assessment activities to support staff development, where appropriate;
- manage the creation of reports (for example for NQTs) so that staff are clear about their progress towards meeting standards and that all information is of a high standard;

- direct and supervise the work of teachers delivering staff development activities;
- lead the production of the Staff Development Handbook and update it regularly;
- provide information and participate in threshold assessment and performance management processes.

The outcomes that are associated with this element are that teachers will:

- have high expectations of all pupils; respect their social, cultural, linguistic, religious and ethnic backgrounds; and are committed to raising their educational achievement;
- treat pupils consistently, with respect and consideration, and are concerned for their development as learners;
- demonstrate and promote the positive values, attitudes and behaviour that they expect from their pupils;
- can communicate sensitively and effectively with parents and carers, recognising their roles in pupils' learning, and their rights, responsibilities and interests in this;
- can contribute to, and share responsibly in, the corporate life of school;
- understand the contribution that support staff and other professionals make to teaching and learning;
- are able to improve their own teaching, by evaluating it, learning from the effective practice of others and from evidence – they are motivated and able to take increasing responsibility for their own professional development;
- are aware of, and work within, the statutory frameworks relating to teachers' responsibilities.

Monitoring and accountability

The tasks that are associated with this element are to:

- provide information, advice and analysis for the headteacher and other senior managers so that they can understand the issues affecting the progress of individuals or groups in the subject;
- monitor, evaluate and review the impact of interventions and resources for staff development;
- respond to other adults and agencies who require up-to-date information about the subject, presented in a concise and accurate manner.

And any other duties as required.

Head of subject

Accountable to: deputy head (quality of teaching) and ultimately the headteacher.

The head of subject is responsible for all aspects of a subject in the school.

Core purpose

The core purpose of a head of subject is to provide professional leadership and management for a subject, to secure high-quality teaching, effective use of resources and improved standards of learning and achievement for all pupils.

Specific tasks

The specific tasks associated with the role of head of subject are:

Leading, managing and developing a subject or curriculum area
The tasks associated with the role of head of subject are specifically to:

- lead the development and implementation of policies and practices in line with school policies;
- advise the headteacher and deputy headteacher of developments in the subject;
- develop and ensure the effective delivery of ICT as part of the subject portfolio;
- prepare development plans as necessary;
- promote the subject in school and beyond;
- participate, where appropriate, in the XXX partnership programme;
- produce reports for the headteacher and deputy headteacher, as required.

The outcomes that are associated with this element are to lead a subject so that teachers will:

- be consistent in their practice;
- be consistent in their implementation of policies;
- use the outcomes of department self-evaluation to develop practice that results in pupil progress;
- collaborate to implement development plans.

The outcomes that are associated with this element are to lead a subject so that pupils will:

- actively participate in learning;
- produce work and assignments in response to curriculum demands (including homework);
- conform to the school's behaviour policy.

The outcomes that are associated with this element are to work as part of the team of heads of subject who:

- are consistent in their practice;
- share good practice with other subject leaders;
- act as role models in teaching pupils effectively;
- act as role models in managing pupils effectively;
- act as role models in demonstrating professional curriculum leadership.

Impact on educational progress of pupils beyond those assigned to the teacher

The outcomes that are associated with this element are to lead the subject so that pupils will:

- achieve high standards in public examinations;
- progress to the next stage of their education with confidence and enthusiasm;
- show sustained improvement in the relevant subject;
- understand how to improve their studies;
- know their academic targets;
- be enthusiastic about the subject;
- contribute to the maintenance of a purposeful working environment.

Leading, developing and enhancing the teaching practice of others and managing staff

The tasks associated with the role of head of subject are specifically to:

- implement school policy on monitoring and evaluating the work of the department – this will include undertaking lesson observation, giving feedback to staff and, where appropriate, setting targets to improve the quality of teaching;

- lead the production and updating of schemes of work – these should ensure curriculum coverage, continuity and progression in the subject for all pupils, including those of high ability and those with special needs;
- coordinate the production of tests and examinations, of the appropriate standard, across the subject area;
- keep parents and carers well informed about their child's achievement in the subject and ensure that all information sent to parents and carers is of a high standard;
- direct and supervise the work of teachers delivering the subject;
- lead the production of the subject handbook and update it regularly;
- provide information and participate in threshold assessment and performance management processes.

The outcomes that are associated with this element are that teachers of the subject will:

- work together as a team with shared aims;
- plan and deliver lessons, using the subject programme of study, where objectives are shared and reviewed;
- support the aims of the school and understand how their team role relates to the school's aims;
- have detailed job descriptions that set out their responsibilities and duties;
- ensure that all pupils are prepared adequately for public examinations;
- keep parents and carers well informed about their child's achievement in the subject and ensure that all information sent to parents and carers is of a high standard;
- monitor the academic progress of the pupils in their teaching groups;
- advise the subject leader on matters affecting the pupils in their groups.

Monitoring and accountability

The tasks that are associated with this element are to:

- provide information, advice and analysis for the headteacher and other senior managers so that they can understand the issues affecting the progress of individuals or groups in the subject;
- monitor, evaluate and review the impact of interventions and resources for the subject;

- respond to other adults and agencies who require up-to-date information about the subject, presented in a concise and accurate manner.

And any other duties as required.

_____ Year leader _____

Accountable to: assistant head (pupil achievement and welfare) and ultimately the headteacher.

Core purpose

- To provide professional leadership and management for a group of pupils to secure high levels of behaviour, promote high levels of ambition and the promotion of independent learning.
- To provide leadership and direction for the year group and ensure that it is managed and organised in such a way to meet the aims and objectives of the school.
- To play a key role in supporting, guiding and motivating pupils, evaluating the effectiveness of the curriculum provision and the outcomes of learning for their year group and progress towards targets, and informing future priorities for their year group.
- To identify needs in their own year group, recognising that these must be considered in relation to the overall needs of the school.

Specific tasks

The specific tasks associated with the role of year leader are:

Leading, managing and developing a cohort of pupils, taking responsibility for pupil development across the curriculum
The outcomes that are associated with this element are to lead a year group so that pupils will:

- attend school regularly and punctually;
- actively participate in learning;
- actively participate in extra-curricular activities;
- produce work and assignments in response to curriculum demands (including homework);

- be safe and happy at school;
- conform to the school's uniform policy;
- conform to the school's behaviour policy.

Impact on educational progress of pupils beyond
those assigned to the teacher
The outcomes that are associated with this element are to lead a year group so that pupils will:

- actively participate in extra-curricular activities;
- achieve high standards in public examinations;
- progress to the next stage of their education with confidence and enthusiasm;
- show sustained improvement across their subjects;
- make informed choices about their future studies;
- understand how to improve their studies;
- know their academic targets;
- show improvement in their literacy, numeracy and information technology skills;
- be well prepared for any tests and examinations;
- be enthusiastic about school;
- contribute to the maintenance of a purposeful working environment.

The outcomes that are associated with this element are to ensure that the teachers and support staff who work with the cohort:

- are well informed about the cohort's targets;
- are well informed about the cohort's progress at the individual and cohort level;
- are challenged and supported where individuals and groups are making insufficient progress.

The outcomes that are associated with this element are to ensure that the parents and carers of the cohort:

- are well informed about their child's achievements at school;
- are well informed about their child's targets for improvement;

- know the expectations made of their child in relation to their studies, their attendance, behaviour and conduct at school;
- know how they can support or assist their child's progress at school.

Leading, developing and enhancing the teaching practice of others and managing staff

The tasks that are associated with this element are to:

- lead a group of tutors who:
  - work together as a tutor team
  - support the aims of the school and understand how their tutor role relates to the school's aims
  - are interested in knowing pupils on a personal level
  - organise activities for pupils
  - monitor the academic progress of the pupils in their tutor group
  - advise the year leader on matters affecting the pupils in their group;
- Work as a team of year leaders who:
  - are consistent in their practice
  - act as role models in managing pupils effectively
  - provide training, development and coaching for staff.

Monitoring and accountability

The tasks that are associated with this element are to:

- provide information and analysis for the headteacher and other senior managers so that they can understand the issues affecting the progress of individuals or groups in each the year group;
- provide advice so that interventions and resources are targeted appropriately;
- monitor, evaluate and review the impact of interventions and resources for the cohort;
- respond to other adults and agencies who require up-to-date information about the pupil, presented in a concise and accurate manner.

And any other duties as required.

Classroom teacher

Core purpose

The core purpose of a classroom teacher is to contribute, as an individual and part of a team, to the realisation of the aims of the school.

We aim to ensure our students:

- enjoy school and thrive in a rich learning environment;
- succeed and achieve their full potential academically, socially, physically and personally;
- learn to make choices as mature citizens in a global society;
- value education as a constant aspect of their lives, enjoying economic well-being;
- make a positive contribution to school and the community as well-mannered representatives of XXX.

We will achieve these aims by:

- providing a high standard of teaching with regular assessment of progress;
- providing a personalised experience where each student learns within a broad, balanced and relevant curriculum;
- requiring all students to behave, dress and work according to the high standards expected;
- providing a consistent disciplined environment where each person willingly complies with the high expectations, enjoys a sense of worth, and is known, valued and respected as an individual;
- ensuring that each student has equal access and every opportunity to make the best use of that education;
- providing an education that will contribute to the spiritual, moral, social and cultural development of our students.

Professional values and practice

The outcomes associated with this element are teachers who:

- have high expectations of all pupils; respect their social, cultural, linguistic, religious and ethnic backgrounds; and are committed to raising their educational achievement;

- treat pupils consistently, with respect and consideration, and are concerned for their development as learners;
- demonstrate and promote the positive values, attitudes and behaviour that they expect from their pupils;
- can communicate sensitively and effectively with parents and carers, recognising their roles in pupils' learning, and their rights, responsibilities and interests in this;
- can contribute to, and share responsibly in, the corporate life of school;
- understand the contribution that support staff and other professionals make to teaching and learning;
- are able to improve their own teaching, by evaluating it, learning from the effective practice of others and from evidence – they are motivated and able to take increasing responsibility for their own professional development;
- are aware of, and work within, the statutory frameworks relating to teachers' responsibilities;
- behave, dress and represent the highest standards of professional conduct at all times.

Knowledge and understanding

Teachers should have a secure knowledge and understanding of the subject(s) they are trained to teach. The outcomes associated with this element are teachers who:

- have an up-to-date knowledge and understanding of their subject and its pedagogy;
- are aware of expectations, typical curricula and teaching arrangements in the key stages or phases before and after the ones they are trained to teach;
- understand how pupils' learning can be affected by their physical, intellectual, linguistic, social, cultural and emotional development;
- know how to use ICT effectively, both to teach their subject and to support their wider professional role;
- understand their responsibilities under the Special Educational Needs Code of Practice, and know how to seek advice from specialists on less common types of special educational needs;

■ know a range of strategies to promote good behaviour and establish a purposeful learning environment.

Teaching: planning, expectations and targets

The outcomes associated with this element are teachers who:

■ set challenging teaching and learning objectives that are relevant to all pupils in their classes, basing these on their knowledge of:

  ■ the pupils

  ■ evidence of their past and current achievement

  ■ the expected standards for pupils of the relevant age range

  ■ the range and content of work relevant to pupils in that age range;

■ use these teaching and learning objectives to plan lessons, and sequences of lessons, showing how they will assess pupils' learning, taking account of and support pupils' varying needs so that girls and boys, from all ethnic groups, can make good progress;

■ select and prepare resources, and plan for their safe and effective organisation, taking account of pupils' interests and their language and cultural backgrounds, with the help of support staff where appropriate;

■ take part in, and contribute to, teaching teams, as appropriate to the school; where applicable, they plan for the deployment of additional adults who support pupils' learning;

■ as relevant to the age range they are trained to teach, are able to plan opportunities for pupils to learn in out-of-school contexts, such as school visits, museums, theatres, fieldwork and employment-based settings, with the help of other staff where appropriate.

Teaching: monitoring and assessment

Teachers should make appropriate use of a range of monitoring and assessment strategies to evaluate pupils' progress towards planned learning objectives, and use this information to improve their own planning and teaching. The outcomes associated with this element are teachers who:

■ monitor and assess as they teach, giving immediate and constructive feedback to support pupils as they learn and involving pupils in reflecting on, evaluating and improving their own performance;

- assess pupils' progress accurately using, as relevant, National Curriculum level descriptions, criteria from national qualifications, the requirements of awarding bodies, National Curriculum and Foundation Stage assessment frameworks or objectives from the national strategies (they may have guidance from an experienced teacher where appropriate);

- identify and support more able pupils, those who are working below age-related expectations, those who are failing to achieve their potential in learning, and those who experience behavioural, emotional and social difficulties (they may have guidance from an experienced teacher where appropriate);

- with the help of an experienced teacher, identify the levels of attainment of pupils learning English as an additional language, analysing the language demands and learning activities in order to provide cognitive challenge as well as language support;

- record pupils' progress and achievements systematically to provide evidence of the range of their work, progress and attainment over time; they use this to help pupils review their own progress and to inform planning;

- use records as a basis for reporting on pupils' attainment and progress orally and in writing, concisely, informatively and accurately for parents, carers, other professionals and pupils.

Teaching and class management

Teachers should have high expectations of pupils and build successful relationships, centred on teaching and learning. They should establish a purposeful learning environment where diversity is valued and where pupils feel secure and confident. All teachers should be able to teach the required or expected knowledge, understanding and skills relevant to the curriculum for pupils in the age range for which they are trained. The outcomes associated with this element are teachers who:

- are punctual to class;
- support school policy on uniform by checking and correcting pupils;
- start the lesson with a register;
- set and assess work according to the school policies;
- have, where appropriate, a seating plan for all classes;

- teach clearly structured lessons or sequences of work that interest and motivate pupils and which:

  - make learning objectives clear to pupils;

  - employ interactive teaching methods and collaborative group work;

  - promote active and independent learning that enables pupils to think for themselves, and to plan and manage their own learning;

- differentiate their teaching to meet the needs of pupils, including the more able and those with special educational needs (they may have guidance from an experienced teacher where appropriate);

- are able to support those who are learning English as an additional language (with the help of an experienced teacher where appropriate);

- take account of the varying interests, experiences and achievements of boys and girls, and pupils from different cultural and ethnic groups, to help pupils make good progress;

- organise and manage teaching and learning time effectively;

- organise and manage the physical teaching space, tools, materials, texts and other resources safely and effectively (with the help of support staff where appropriate);

- set high expectations for pupils' behaviour and establish a clear framework for classroom discipline to anticipate and manage pupils' behaviour constructively, and promote self-control and independence;

- use ICT effectively in their teaching;

- take responsibility for teaching a class or classes over a sustained and substantial period of time, teaching across the age and ability range for which they are trained;

- provide homework and other out-of-class work that consolidates and extends work carried out in the class and encourages pupils to learn independently;

- work collaboratively with specialist teachers and other colleagues and, with the help of an experienced teacher as appropriate, manage the work of teaching assistants or other adults to enhance pupils' learning;

- recognise and respond effectively to equal opportunities issues as they arise in the classroom, including by challenging stereotyped views, and by challenging bullying or harassment, following relevant policies and procedures.

And any other duties as required.

Curriculum administrator

Accountable to: PA2, business manager and ultimately the headteacher.

- Grade: 6 (points 18–21).
- Hours: 37 hours per week over 39 weeks (term time plus five days by arrangement) 8.30 a.m.–4.30 p.m. (Monday to Thursday); 8.00 a.m.–3.30 p.m. (Friday).
- Lunch: 30 minutes per day, unpaid – by arrangement with line manager (staff room is available).

Core purpose

- To provide supervision for the classes of absent staff and administrative support for subject departments.
- To identify needs in their role and recognise that these must be considered in relation to the overall needs of the school.

Specific tasks

The specific tasks and responsibilities associated with the role of curriculum administrator are:

- to supervise classes for absent staff;
- to receive the work from the cover manager and to ensure that all students are given the work to do;
- to take the attendance register for the classes supervised;
- to complete the class supervision report for the PA to the deputy heads;
- to undertake administrative support for teachers, as determined by the PA to the deputy heads;
- to report any incidents involving students to the PA to the deputy heads;
- to take responsibility for keeping the administration area tidy (as part of the 'clean desk policy');
- to assist, where needed, in the hospitality for guests and visitors;
- to act as a member of the general office team, assisting with duties as and when necessary;
- to provide administrative support to the teaching staff, including filing, preparation of teaching materials, classroom displays, stocktaking, maintaining department records, etc.;
- other duties as required.

empowerment, 112–13
  problem solving, 141–2
  progression through, 42–7
  supporting, 43, 46, 54
  tutoring, 43, 45–6, 48–50, 52–3, 54
competencies:
  administration team, 108–9
  Fast Track candidates, 165
  focus performance management, 113
  Hay McBer, 22, 122–3
  individuals, 166
  leadership, 10–11, 122–3, 165–6
  organisations, 166
complaints/grievances, 32–3
Conditions of Employment (Part XII, STPCD), 59–61
confidentiality, 31–2
consistent practice, 2, 10–11
contextual value-added, 89
counsellors, 2
cover assistants, 2
Covey, Stephen, 55
Crainer, S. and Dearlove, D., 166
criticism see feedback
culture of schools, 106
  changes to, 2–15, 40, 116
curriculum:
  administration, 2, 188–9
  planning, 19, 45

Department for Health: Organisation Policy, 18–19
Developing Leaders Programme (Specialist Schools Trust), 154
DfES, 89
  definition of performance management, 6–8
  Performance Management in Schools (2000), 4–6
  relationship with schools, 85–6
  and teacher workload, 35
dialogue, 142–3
directive behaviour, 43
director of staff development: job description, 172–6
distributed leadership, 63
domains of practice, 157

Edenborough, R., 163
Education (School Teacher Appraisal) Regulations (1991), 82
examination administrators, 2

Exceptions Report, 89
expectations of others, 146–7
external adviser (EA), 86, 88, 94
  role, 83–5

Fast Track programme, 141, 161–2
  assessment techniques, 164
  competencies and behaviours, 165
feedback:
  entitlement to, 168
  negative, 33
    providing sensitively, 151–2, 160
    sensitivity to, 46
  peer, 139table
  on staff development activities, 156
  student, 137–8
  360-degree, 136–40
    peer, 138–40, 139table
    proforma, 139–40
  success criteria, 137
Fischer Family Trust (FFT), 88–9
Five Year Strategy for Children and Learners, 168–9
Form 7, 44
formal annual review, 128–36 see also appraisals; performance management; performance review
  challenges, 130–2
  of committed staff member, 130–3
  content, 132–3
  identifying areas for development, 130–2
  lesson observation, 20, 34–5, 128, 134, 136, 160
  reviewing previous objectives, 130
  statement:
    areas for development, 136
    clarity, 136
    focus on data, 136
    and objectives, 132–3
  and threshold standards, 22, 31, 120–2, 128, 143
  of underachieving staff member, 134–6

GCSEs, 89
goals see objectives; targets
governing body, 20
governors, 86, 87
  head teacher performance management, 82–5, 94
Green Book, 98

Hay McBer:
  competencies, 22
    for school leadership, 122–3
  leadership model, 166–7
  Models of Excellence for Schools (2001),
    166
head of department, 61–2
  performance review meeting,
    125–7
    agenda, 124–5
  professional characteristics, 122–3
  Singapore, 165
head of faculty, 61–2
head of subject:
  job description, 177–80
  National Standards (TTA), 166
head of year, 62
  accountability, 182
  core purpose, 69
  disciplinary role, 99–102
  job description, 70–1, 76, 180–2
head teacher, 15
  appraisal, 82
  competencies, 122–3
  core purpose, 68–9, 161
  National Standards (TTA), 166
  performance management, 82–5,
    94–5
    external advisor (EA), 83–5
    frequency of reviews, 90
    responsibility, 86
    review panel, 83–5
    setting objectives, 87–90
high-performing staff member: formal
    annual review, 130–3
  statement, 132–3

implementation: performance
    procedures, 117–23
independent consultants, 86
individuals: core competencies, 166
induction programmes, 11
  coaching model, 107
  targets, 107
information sharing, 6
INSET sessions, 146
  developing programme, 35
  principles of, 153–4
  and school improvement plan, 157
  and staff development, 153–4
  whole-school benefits, 156–7
institutional objectives, 15
IT technicians, 2

jargon, 107
job construction:
  grading, 67–8
  identifying core purpose, 68–70
  pay, 67–8, 78
  and school improvement plan,
    64–7
job descriptions:
  assessment administrator, 103–4
  bursar, 77
  classroom teacher, 183–7
  curriculum administrator, 188–9
  director of staff dvelopment, 172–6
  for distinct roles, 77
  effective, 61
  head of subject, 76, 177–80
  head of year, 70–1, 76, 180–2
  headings, 78
  level of pay, 78
  methodology for producing, 77–8
  outcomes, 70–1
  with performance objectives, 71–2
  personal assistants, 76
  purpose, 58, 76–7
  secretaries, 76
  specific tasks and responsibilities,
    70–1
  statutory guidance, 58–9
  Stoll model, 77
  support staff, 75–7
  titles, 61–7, 77
    choosing, 63–4
    terminology, 61–3
  and TLR allowances, 72

Kelly, Ruth, 86
key stage results, 28

Labour government (2001–5), 85–6
leadership:
  assessment of potential, 162–4
  distributed, 63
  models:
    competency, 165–6
    Hay McBer, 166–7
    National Standards, 166–7
  programmes, 161–5
    and performance management,
      161
  situational, 43*figure*
  team, 15
    meetings, 41–2
  tenacity, 51

leadership (*cont'd*)
  transactional, 167
  transformational, 166–7
LEAs:
  and head teacher appraisal, 82
  link adviser, 86
legal/statutory issues:
  complaints about review process,
    32–3
  framework for performance
    management, 2, 4, 20
  pay reviews, 28
  schools, 20, 106
Legatt, T.: characteristics of teaching
    profession, 98–9
lesson observation, 3, 20, 134
  and formal annual review, 128
  inertia, 160
  Ofsted framework, 34
  policy on, 34–5
  reports, 35
  training, 136
lessons: Ofsted criteria for excellence,
    34
LfM (Leading from the Middle), 154
line manager: role, 7
link adviser, 82, 86

management:
  allowances, 67 (*see also* TLR
    allowance (teaching and
    learning responsibility))
  assessment, 102–4, 103–4
  behaviour, 99–102
  change, 117–18
  paradigms, 14
    collegial, 62
    hierarchical, 61–2
Maslow's hierarchy of needs, 12–13,
    12*figure*
meetings, 3 *see also* performance
    review
  agendas, 124–5, 127, 134–5
  dialogue, 134–5
  effective, 55–6
  inertia, 160
  leadership team, 41–2
  new starters and, 42
  one-to-one, 40–2, 168
    agenda, 127
    effective, 52
    role, 40–2, 47
  preparation, 134–5

record-keeping, 56, 126–8, 129*table*,
    135, 160
  underachieving staff member,
    134–5
mission statement, 20–1
monitoring progress, 5, 7, 90–4
motivation, 12–14
  hygiene theory, 13
  Maslow's hierarchy of needs,
    12–13, 12*figure*
  and performance management,
    13

NASUWT, 87
National Agreement *see Raising
    Standards and Tackling Workload*
    National Agreement
National College for School
    Leadership (NCSL), 161
National Professional Qualification for
    Headship (NPQH), 43
National Standards (DfES), 22
  head teacher, 68–9
  professional characteristics, 122
National Standards (TTA), 166
New Relationship with Schools, 84,
    85–6, 170
new starters:
  meetings and, 42
  newly qualified teachers (NQTs),
    141
  support staff, 105–7
non-contact time, 98, 99
NPQH (National Professional
    Qualification for
    Headteachers), 154

objectives, 20, 26 *see also* targets
  agreeing, 7, 29–31
  aligning staff with, 140–2
  central role, 160–1
  data for setting, 88–90
  head teacher, 87–90
  institutional, 15
  monitoring, 90–4
  and outcomes, 88
  performance management, 168–9
  prior attainment baseline, 88
  and review statement, 132–3
  setting, 5
Ofsted, 43, 89
  criteria for lesson excellence, 34
  curriculum planning, 45

Ofsted (cont'd)
  framework for lesson observations, 34
  impact, 50
one-to-one meetings, 40–2, 168
  agenda, 127
  effective, 52
  role, 40–2, 47
Optical Mark Reader (OMR), 102
organisations:
  consistency, 142
  core competencies, 166
outcomes:
  access to, 32
  bursar, 77
  curriculum administrator, 189
  head of subject, 76, 177–9
  head of year, 76, 181–2
  and objectives, 88
  and performance criteria, 77
  personal assistant roles, 76
  quantifiable, 166
  secretarial role, 76

para-professionals, 2
pastoral welfare, 62
pay see also TLR allowance (teaching and learning responsibility)
  factors influencing level, 78
  head teacher's, 85
  and performance review, 6, 24–5, 28, 30–1
  support staff, 98
  teachers, 98
peer review:
  feedback, 138–40, 139table
    resistance to, 4
  proforma, 138–40
Performance and Assesment Report (PANDA), 84, 88, 89
performance management, 6–8
  see also appraisals; formal annual review; performance review
  commitment, 4
  continuous/flexible, 136–7
  cycle, 6–7, 29–31, 119figure
  defined, 6–8, 143
  effective, 20–1, 142, 146
  entitlement to, 168
  framework, 11–12
  key steps, 4–6
  legal framework, 20

monitoring progress, 5, 7, 90–4
reviewing achievements, 7
risks, 160–1
roles, 25–7
and school improvement planning cycle, 117–18, 120table
Performance Management in Schools (DfES, 2000), 4–6
performance review, 5 see also appraisals; formal annual review; performance management
  criteria: and outcomes, 77
  dimensions, 21–2
  evaluating, 7
  feedback, 33
  importance, 152–3
  introducing, 123–8
  knowledge and understanding, 120–1
  link to threshold standards, 143
  meetings, 3 (see also meetings)
    agendas, 124–5, 127, 134–5
    dialogue, 127–8
    head of department, 125–7
    preparation, 135
    record-keeping, 126–8, 129table
    underachieving staff member, 134–5
  objectives:
    head teacher, 87–90
    and job descriptions, 71–2
  panel, 83–5
  and pay, 24–5, 30–1
    link to, 6, 31
  personal development, 122
  professional characteristics, 122–3
  responsibilities, 27–8
  schedule, 5
  sharing information, 6
  summary, 116
  support staff, 112–13
  teaching and assessment, 121
  and threshold standards, 22, 31, 120–2, 128, 143
  timimg, 28–9
personal development, 122
PLASC, 44
policies on performance management, 31
  access to outcomes, 32
  areas needing, 18–19
  commitment to, 4

policies on performance management
(*cont'd*)
  complaints/grievances, 32–3
  components, 33–4
  confidentiality, 31–2
  defining roles, 4
  development process, 21–5
  documents, 5
  effectiveness, 6, 33
  elements, 23–34
  on information sharing, 6
  on lesson observation, 34–5
  links with other policies, 31
  on monitoring progress, 5
  Organisation Policy (DfH), 18–19
  and pay, 6
  purpose, 18, 20, 23–4
  responsibilites of participants, 5
  setting objectives, 5
  timetable for review process, 5
  weak performance, 31
  working group, 22–3
PPA (planning, preparation and
    assessment), 9, 98, 99
PricewaterhouseCoopers (PwC) report,
    35
primary schools: SIPs, 86
prior attainment, 88, 89
professionalism, 2–3, 14–15
  characteristics, 122–3
  increasing, 168–9
  National Standards (DfES), 122
  1970s analysis, 51
  perceived attack on, 4
  teachers concept of, 51
  trait model, 98–9
  values and practice, 183–4
progress, 11
  monitoring, 5, 90–4
  pupil, 20, 28
psychometric testing, 163
pupil experience: and INSET sessions,
    153
pupil learning assistants, 2
pupil progress, 20, 28
  and teacher performance, 29

qualified teacher status (QTS):
    National Standards (TTA), 166

Raising Standards and Tackling Workload
    National Agreement, 8–9, 36,
    67

record-keeping, 56
  importance, 135
  inertia, 160
  performance review meetings,
    126–8, 129*table*
residual analysis, 130–1*figures*
review statement *see* formal annual
    review, statement
risks, 160–1
role playing: developing
    self-reflection, 146–51
Ruskin College, 14

salary review *see* pay
school improvement partner (SIP),
    85–7, 88, 94–5
school improvement plan, 84
  aligning staff with, 140–2
  and INSET sessions, 153, 157
  and performance management
    cycle, 117–18, 120*table*
School Information Management
    System (SIMS), 102
school secretary, 2
School Teachers' Pay and Conditions
    Document (STPCD), 59–61, 85
schools:
  aims, 20–1
  basis for improvement, 168–9
  collegial model, 62
  culture, 66, 106
    changes to, 2–15, 116
  development plan, 41, 122
  dynamics (Stoll model), 64–7
  hierarchical model, 61–2
  history, 66
  and individual performance, 29
  legal framework, 20, 106
  micro-politics, 63–4, 66
  mission statement, 20–1
  monitoring:
    successful, 93–4
    underachieving, 90–3
  morale, 66
  performance analysis, 88–9
  primary: SIPs, 86
  projected performance, 88–9
  relationships within, 65–6
  results analysis, 84
  secondary:
    attainment data, 89
    non-contact time, 98, 99
    SIPs, 86

schools: (cont'd)
  structures, 66
  student mix, 65
  successful, 93–4
  underachieving, 90–3
science technicians, 2
SDR: Top Talent programme, 162–4
secondary schools:
  attainment data, 89
  non-contact time, 98, 99
  SIPs, 86
Section 10 inspection reports, 84
self-evaluation form (SEF), 84
self-reflection/internal review process:
    stimulating, 146–51
shared planning, 2, 10–11
Sim v. Rotherham MBC (1986), 58–9
SIMS Form 7 module, 44
Singapore: Ministry of Education,
  165
single conversation, 86
situational leadership, 43figure
16PF (Cattell), 163
special educational need coordinators
  (SENCO): National Standards
  (TTA), 166
Special Educational Needs (SEN)
  Code of Practice, 89
staff development, 3, 20, 146 see also
  coaching
  coaching and, 40–2, 156–7
  components, 155–6
  costs, 154
  feedback, 156
  identifying needs, 31
  and INSET sessions, 153–4
  link to performance management,
    152–7, 161
  modelling and demonstrations, 155
  and organisational goals, 157
  outcomes, 173–5
  planning activities, 155–6
  role of meetings, 40–2
  theory presentation, 155
  training, 11
  workshops, 156
standards, 11, 21–2
  threshold, 22, 31, 120–2, 128, 143
Stoll, L.: learning context model,
  64–7
STPCD, 67
successful schools: monitoring, 93–4

support staff:
  administration team, 109–11table
  assessment administrator, 103–4
  communicating and influencing, 108
  conditions of service, 98
  continuous improvement, 108
  counsellors, 2
  cover assistants, 2
  curriculum administrator, 2, 188–9
  development needs, 9–10
  effective behaviours, 108–12
  examination administrators, 2
  identifying roles, 99–103
  induction, 105–7
  initiative, 109
  interface with classroom life, 106
  IT technicians, 2
  location criteria, 104–5
  management needs, 9–10
  managing performance, 105
  need for, 8–9, 36, 75–7, 98–9
  pay, 98
  performance review, 112–13
  proactive approach, 108–9
  problem solving and judgement, 109
  and school jargon, 107
  school secretary, 2
  science technicians, 2
  student management, 106–7
  teamwork, 109
  work space, 104
supportive behaviour, 43
synergy, 55

talent-spotting, 161–4
targets see also objectives
  academic, 70–1
  head's, 118
  induction programmes, 107
  performance, 30–1
  performance management, 31
  target-setting, 118
  whole-school, 118
teachers see also professionalism
  assessment management: role,
    102–3
  career progression, 164
  class management, 186–7
  classroom:
    core purpose, 69
    disciplinary role, 100–2
    job descriptions, 183–7

teachers *see also* professionalism (*cont'd*)
  coaching and, 156–7
  conditions of service, 59–61, 98
  development needs, 7
  job descriptions, 183–7
  knowledge and understanding,
    184–5
  monitoring and assessing pupils,
    185–6
  need for performance management,
    2–8
  newly appointed, 58
  newly qualified (NQTs), 141
  non-contact time, 98
  pay, 98
  performance: and school as-a-
    whole, 29
  planning, 185
  support, 2, 15
  team leader:
    accountability, 11
    competencies, 10–11
  workload, 8–9, 36, 67
    DfES policy, 35
    reducing, 35–6
*Teacher's Rights, Duties and
  Responsibilities*, 58–9
teaching assistants, 2
Teaching and Learning Review,
  169
teaching quality *see* lesson
  observations
team leaders, 15
  accountability, 11
  competencies, 10–11
  role, 167–8
teams, 15
  core values, 76
teamwork: definition, 167
Theory X, 14
Theory Y, 14
360-degree feedback, 136–40
  peer, 138–40, 139*table*
    pro forma, 139–40

  from students, 137–8
  success criteria, 137
threshold assessment, 24
threshold standards, 22, 31
  framework for formal annual
    review, 128
  link to performance review system,
    143
  model for performance reviews,
    120–2
TLR allowance (teaching and learning
    responsibility), 10, 73–4*tables*,
    77 *see also* pay
  determining, 67–8
  head of year, 70
  and job descriptions, 72–5
  and performance review, 72
Top Talent programme, 162–4
training and development *see* staff
    development
Tranter, S., 161

underachieving schools: monitoring,
    90–3
underachieving staff member:
  developing dialogue, 135
  formal annual review, 134–6
  identifying areas for development,
    135–6
unions, 87
  and policy development, 24–5

vision, alignment of, 46, 48–50

Watson-Glaser Critical Thinking
    Appraisal Test, 163
West, M. and Allen, N., 167
work team, 167
workforce reform, 35–6
working group, 117
  managing, 24–5
  policy, 22–3
  roles of members, 24–5

Outcomes

The outcomes that are associated with this specific role are to work as part of the team of curriculum administrators who:

- are consistent in their practice;
- share good practice with others;
- act as role models in managing clients effectively;
- act as role models in demonstrating professional administrative support.

The outcomes associated with being a member of the administration team is that there is:

- effective communication;
- a proactive approach to meeting the needs of stakeholders;
- an individual and team belief in continuous improvement, which is evidenced through activity;
- planned and coordinated work schedules;
- effective management of problems;
- effective teamwork, where everyone is treated with dignity and respect.